RELATIONSHIPS AND SEXUALITY

CARMEL WYNNE

MERCIER PRESS

DEDICATION

This book is dedicated to Colm, my best friend, husband and lover, with deepest love and appreciation for all your support and encouragement.

First published in 1997 by
Mercier Press
PO Box 5, 5 French Church Street,
Cork
16 Hume Street Dublin 2
Trade enquiries to CMD Distribution
55A Spruce Avenue Stillorgan Industrial
Park Blackrock County Dublin

© Carmel Wynne 1997

ISBN 1 85635 185 8

10 9 8 7 6 5 4 3 2 1

A CIP record for this title is available
from the British Library

Cover design by
Penhouse Design Group
Set by Richard Parfrey
Printed in Ireland by ColourBooks,
Baldoyle Industrial Estate, Dublin 13

Published in the U.S. and Canada by
the Irish American Book Company,
6309 Monarch Park Place, Niwot,
Colorado, 80503.
Telephone (303) 530-1352, (800) 452-7115.
Fax (303) 530-4488, (800) 401-9705.

ACKNOWLEDGEMENTS

Without the love, encouragement and patience of my family I could not have managed to make the time to write this book. Thank you, Colm, for accepting me exactly as I am and for your support in everything I do. Thank you for all the fun and pleasure we shared as we learned how to be parents. Thank you, Aileen, for asking the right questions. Your natural childish curiosity was the spur that sent me out to become more knowledgeable about sex education. I want to thank Niamh for her ability to stay calm and her refusal ever to panic with me – regardless of the crisis. Thank you, Deirdre-Anne, for your friendly interest in my writing progress and for your integrity. Your views on the role of mothers challenged me to clarify my thinking about family commitments. Thank you, Aoife-Marie, for being such a positive person. I appreciate your lovely ability to build your family and your friends up. You help others to be more confident without putting them under any pressure. You have shown great courage in overcoming calamity and making a fresh start.

I also want to thank my family of origin: my late father George, my mother Nora Meehan, my sister Monnie and my brothers Pat, Joe and Martin for teaching me how powerfully our early relationships affect us all our lives. Each one of you has been important in helping me to expand my understanding of family interactions.

Many other wonderful people have played a part in my life and have unknowingly been instrumental in the

4

preparation and writing of this book. I started to write when Toni Smith invited me to submit scripts for *Nightlight*, an RTÉ programme. Without your intervention, Toni, I might never have discovered that I had the ability to write and be published. Thank you so much. I am particularly grateful to Angela MacNamara for her invitation to me to work in relationships and sexuality education. Without your incredibly generous encouragement, support and guidance, Angela, I would not have had the courage to do this work. I am also very appreciative of the role played by Margaret Martin who did the research for my *Late Late Show* interview with Gay Byrne. This book was written as a result of the overwhelming response to that interview.

I am grateful to my daughter Niamh for demanding sexual equality from a very early age. When a priest told her she could not be an altar server because she was a girl, she told me he was wrong. At ten years of age she pushed me into reviewing my own attitudes to sexual equality and the role of women. My quest for answers to her provocative questions led me to query repressive church teaching and study theology. I owe an enormous debt of gratitude to Brid O'Connell, David Weakliam O Carm. and especially to Michael Gallagher SJ, who helped me in my spiritual quest.

I will always be grateful for the ways in which special friends Mary Kavanagh, Joyce O'Hara, Therese O'Reilly, Mary Sexton and Jess Walshe have touched and enriched my life. I am so grateful that I have known and loved each of you. Thank you especially to Ciaran Cavanagh and Margaret Byrne, two unique people who have the rare ability to truly listen. I remember with gratitude the many times you were there for me when I needed a listening ear, a shoulder to cry on or a challenge to stop feeling sorry for myself.

I also want to thank two other wonderful people who believed in me and pushed me gently to do more risky but challenging work. Thank you Bernie Rossney for calming me with encouraging phone calls and for your quiet wisdom. Thank you Gay Waterstone, my soulmate and dearest friend. You make a great ally when our partners Colm and Desmond are 'stirring the pot'. I also want to thank Anne Weakliam and Marion Ó Cléirigh for introducing me to the life-changing philosophy of Anthony de Mello SJ, the greatest spiritual master of this century. I particularly want to thank John Callanan SJ, teacher and friend. I have no doubt that your honest evaluations have dared me to move out of my comfort zones. Thank you for the precious gift of your friendship and for your ongoing support in my work.

Thank you to Brendan Byrne, Margrit Cruickshank, Roisin Conroy, Caroline Liddy, Aidan O'Hara, Sean Spellissey and Bernadette Wynne who offered advice and support while I was writing this book. A special word of thanks to Ella Shanahan, editor of the 'Education and Living' supplement of the *Irish Times*, who allowed me to use material from my published articles in this book. Thank you also to Jo O'Donoghue, my publisher in Mercier Press.

I want to thank the wonderful girls and boys, in both primary and post-primary schools, who had the courage to ask truthful questions about what young people really need to know. I appreciate your honesty and feel very privileged that so many of you help to keep me up to date. Thank you for discussing your points of view so openly and for listening with respect to mine. I have learned a great deal about effective relationships and sexuality education from your suggestions. I particularly want to express my gratitude to the classes who gave me permission to use their questions and quote from their comments.

CONTENTS

AUTHOR'S NOTE

In order to avoid the awkwardness of 's/he', 'his or her' and other such pronoun complications, throughout the text the recipient of the information will be 'he' and the informing parent or teacher 'she', unless the context clearly requires gender specificity.

INTRODUCTION

Over the last few years I have had numerous requests
from parents and teachers who heard me give talks or
read my newspaper and magazine articles to write a book
on the subject of relationships and sexuality education.
After Gay Byrne interviewed me on the *Late Late Show* in
March 1996, the number of requests grew to a flood. Total
strangers who recognised me from the show stopped me
in the street to talk and ask for advice. Almost everyone
I spoke to was aware of the sexual pressures on girls and
boys. They just did not know what to do about it. The
same questions and comments came up in these conversations time and time again.

- 'When and how do we talk to our children about sex?'
- 'I'm too embarrassed to talk to my child' or 'My child
  is too embarrassed to talk to me.'
- 'How can we find a language that is not too clinical in
  talking about sex?'
- 'Should you tell them about contraception or is that
  only encouraging them?'
- 'Can we do anything to stop adolescent girls and boys
  having sex?'
- 'Adults need sex education more than the children.'

This book sets out to address these questions and
respond to these comments – and many more.

As soon as children are old enough to ask questions
they are old enough to have these questions answered. If

adults are embarrassed or seek to avoid answering these questions the child picks this up. He senses that there is something wrong with asking how the body works, where babies come from, why Sarah's baby has no daddy and other such questions.

For some lucky children sex education is a normal part of growing up. Others belong in families where sex is a taboo subject. These learn about sex from their peers or the media. Regardless of how they first learn about human reproduction, all young people discuss the matter with their friends. Often they swap garbled half-truths and distorted stories about sexual behaviour. One result of picking up information like this is that it leaves the recipients with complicated feelings about sex – excitement, embarrassment, fear and shame. The moral dimension is often left out entirely or dismissed as old-fashioned.

Newspaper and television coverage of abuse may introduce some children to aberrant sex. The result is that they worry, especially when they hear discussions about child sexual abuse, but some never ask parents for the information that would reassure them. One reason is that they do not have the language to ask for explanations. It is the worst possible way for children to learn about sex, and parents may be totally unaware of how they may be affected. They assume the topics go over the head of the child but they are wrong. Adults cannot protect children from seeing news reports of rape, incest or child sexual abuse, or hearing these issues discussed on talk shows. Youngsters sense the distaste and repulsion adults experience at such horrific happenings. They know something terrible has happened to do with sexual experience but they may be unsure what exactly is terrible. There is a danger that they will begin to associate sex with something dirty, unpleasant or even dangerous. Children may also be curious and excited when they hear adults laugh at sexy jokes they do not understand. The truth about sex education is that many young people, *in every generation*, are brought up in families who do not have the skills to educate them positively about sexuality. Adults who feel they themselves need sex education have a sound instinct. Sex education is a lifelong process and children can help in this learning if adults listen to them.

People can do nothing to change the means by which they first learned about sex but they have choices about whether to allow that early information to affect their adult relationships. They can choose, too, whether to educate their own children in the way they were educated or in a different way. My belief is that the vast majority of parents want to do it differently. We are fortunate today to have psychological insights that will help us learn about relationships in ways our parents never knew and therefore could not teach. Family relationships are only as good as family communication, and children learn relationship skills by imitating how their parents communicate with each other. Psychological research has established that only 7 per cent of communication has to do with words. The other 93 per cent has to do with facial expression, body language and tone of voice.

If parents allow each other *honestly* to express all their feelings, positive as well as negative, the child learns to communicate honestly. If parents listen to each other with respect, the child learns trust. He learns that it is OK to talk about *all* his feelings. He learns it is acceptable to talk to his parents about anything. In fact the majority of girls and boys are brought up in families that do not have these communication skills. The parents are not to blame in this. How can they teach their children skills that they have not learned from their parents? If grandparents had repressed attitudes to sexuality they may have passed these on to parents. They in their turn passed them on to their children. Unless some new learning takes place, skills deficits are passed down from generation to generation.

For the most part our culture does not teach children how to communicate honestly and with loving respect. As a society, too, we lack clarity about our sexual values. I firmly believe that any adult or adolescent who has high self-esteem will have an instinctive understanding of how casual sex could damage him physically, emotionally and spiritually. He will not need to be discouraged or told not to have sex; he will know how to make responsible choices naturally.

Research evidence shows that a great deal of sexual experimentation is a vain attempt by young people to find in sex the love and reassurance and affection they do not experience at home. Parents and teachers regularly ask me such questions as, 'How do you stop young people having sex?' or 'How do you discourage young people from becoming sexually active?' If I am answering a teacher I say, 'You begin by trying to discover the attitudes the child has picked up from the sex education that is done in the home.' If I am talking to a parent (who is usually a mother) I say, 'You have already done a lot to influence your child's decision by the way you show your love for your partner and how you communicate love to your child.'

If I am giving a talk to a group of parents in a school and I have enough time I might suggest that asking 'How do you stop them having sex?' is the wrong question. A better question might be: 'How can I teach my child to have the self-esteem and self-respect he needs to be a loving, caring person, a person who has a proper understanding of sexual intimacy?' When I elaborate on the topic I am often told, 'You should write a book.' So for all those extraordinarily kind people who have asked me to write, here is that book.

1

RETHINKING SEX EDUCATION

NOT TELLING

A small number of parents believe that it is not good to tell a child about the facts of life before puberty. One fear is that too much information too soon will encourage an inappropriate curiosity about sex. It is easy to understand why caring adults want children to be protected and kept innocent for as long as possible. No one wants a child to miss out on childhood pleasures. The desire to allow girls and boys enjoy their childhood instead of encouraging them to become mini-adults is commendable.

The right of a parent to protect a child in whatever way she thinks is best must always be respected. However, it cannot be denied that a small number of adults who want to safeguard the innocence of children do so by denying them information. They deliberately set out to keep them ignorant of the facts of sex. Innocence must never be confused with ignorance. Innocence is freedom from guilt; ignorance is a lack of information. When families deny information and adopt a 'we-don't-talk-about-these-things' attitude to obvious questions, about genital differences between the sexes for example, children may get the wrong impression. They sense the discomfort and assume that sexual matters are taboo and not to be talked about with family members. Sometimes the very desire to protect a child has the opposite effect to that intended. The child gets the message that his interest is disapproved of and wrongly assumes that knowing about sex is bad.

There is no denying that some adults who avoid answering a child's questions are unconsciously protecting themselves from embarrassment. Some of these admit that they need guidance on how to talk to children of different ages about sexuality. They worry that they do not have the right information or the correct language and will not be able to answer questions. While most people welcome the greater openness that now exists in our society, it deeply worries others. The liberal approach to sexuality concerns parents who want to pass on their more traditional values to their children.

CHANGED TIMES

Adults no longer have control over their children's environment in the way they used to. In less than twenty years the pendulum seems to have swung from one extreme to the other, from unhealthy sexual repression to promiscuous sexual freedom. One reason for this enormous change is the influence of television and videos. This generation of children is being sexually educated by the media, whereas many of their parents were kept ignorant of the facts of life until puberty. It seemed easier then. Comics and books written for children were full of

harmless fun and mischief; radio and television programmes produced for youngsters rarely dealt with
controversial topics. Teenagers did not have access to
sexy videos or violently explicit films. Although girls and
boys were naturally curious about passion and love they
had fewer sources of information. Those who actively
sought information about sex found this information in
medical books and dictionaries. It was easy enough to get
information about the mechanics of physical sex but most
remained ignorant of the emotional and spiritual dimensions
of relationships.

This protective environment was not ideal, nor is the
current permissive environment that makes commercial
use of sexually explicit imagery to sell products. It may
not be wise for a parent to base a judgement on what kind
of sex education to give a child on her own childhood
experiences. There is no comparison between the world
in which parents grew up and that in which children are
growing up today. It is foolish if not irresponsible to try
to keep a child ignorant of the facts of life. Nor is it ever
right to lie to children about the matter, although some
parents in the past did so in a misguided attempt to
protect innocence. It is a sign of dysfunction in a family
if such important subjects are not spoken about.

I suspect that many people would rethink their attitudes to sex education if they fully realised how powerful
media influences are in shaping attitudes to sex and
intimacy. Even if a child is not allowed to watch television
he cannot be protected from the sexual imagery in
window displays, in magazine and card shops and bill-
board advertisements. Whether adults like it or not, young

people are being fed a diet of instant romance and immediate gratification by media sources. One result of this is that children are given unrealistic expectations about intimacy once they become sexually curious at puberty. The belief that sex will be uninhibited, spontaneous and earth-shattering *the first time* is widespread among adolescents. Some adults may also buy into this myth and carry the disappointment of having missed out in their youth.

Of course it is healthy for teenagers to want their first experience to be with someone really special. However, it is worrying that so many have expectations of having several sexual partners. Many young people are honest enough to admit that they do not expect to marry the first person with whom they have sex, and good sex education should make young people aware of the serious risks attached to engaging in sex with different partners.

MEDIA EXPLICITNESS

Television soaps are generally watched by the whole family and many of them show simulated sexual activity. Parents should not assume that children are ignorant about what is going on. Girls and boys can learn about pregnancy and childbirth from appropriately made documentary programmes. On the other hand they may also learn about sexual problems and perverted sexual behaviour if a parent is not vigilant. If a child is playing in the room when a parent or child-minder is watching an afternoon chat show, he may hear adult discussions on the most intimate details of people's sexual lives, which often involve perverted experiences. Recently I met some parents who were shocked to discover girls as young as eight or nine years old putting Barbie and Ken dolls naked into bed together. When asked to explain what they were doing the children said things like: 'They are sexing', 'They are having a sex' and 'They are going to make a baby.'

Some children clearly understand what adults do in bed. Many know someone personally who is cohabiting – a relation, schoolfriend's parent or a neighbour. It is hardly surprising that children tend to accept that couples who fall in love have sex regardless of whether they are married or not. Books and magazines written for teenagers contain sexually explicit material that would have been considered outrageous even a decade ago. The problem pages of most teenage magazines advise young people that pre-marital sex is all right as long as the couple love each other and have 'safe sex'. The spirituality of sexuality is nearly always ignored. Without a positive appreciation of how sexual love affects the body, mind and spirit, young people will never learn to have a holistic approach to sexuality.

Most popular television soaps deal with real-life issues. They explore painful relationship situations and bring into the open family problems that used to remain hidden. Teenage pregnancy, abortion, incest, extra-marital relationships, wife battering, surrogate motherhood and homosexuality have all been dealt with in the more popular programmes. Very few parents take the opportunity to talk to young people about these issues. When parents comment and share their views they can challenge attitudes to relationships and sexuality that do not fit in with their own values.

Children as young as twelve years old read magazines that are supposedly marketed for older teenagers. They could educate their parents about the variety of positions one can use during lovemaking. American parents find it is so difficult to exercise control over children's television viewing that they need a V-chip, a piece of computer technology that enables a parent to programme a television set to go blank when explicit material is displayed on the screen. A similar chip may also be needed in Europe. Film clips that advertise sexually explicit evening movies are often shown on daytime TV. British and Irish children are watching the same Australian and American soaps as their counterparts on those continents. Children who hear discussions of sexual scandals on radio and television may if they are paying attention find these events disturbing. They know they have something to do with sex which then becomes associated in their minds with something terrible. If no one explains why adults are so scandalised, children cannot help thinking that sex is dirty or unpleasant. The experience leaves them feeling both uncomfortable and confused and encourages a negative attitude to sex.

If a young child hears a discussion on deviant sex on the radio or television it must not be assumed that what he saw or heard has gone over his head. A concerned parent becomes attuned to picking up anxious questions even if they are not phrased as questions. Younger children cannot talk about what bothers them the way older children and adults can. Sometimes even teenagers do not have the language or vocabulary to express their fears and concerns.

INDIRECT QUESTIONS

The concerned parent should seek to discover what is behind indirect questions. For example, 'Why is Marie so late?' sounds simple but it could be a sign of the need for safety and reassurance. A good way for the parent to help is to focus on the worry for a moment and see if she can identify what exactly is troubling the child before offering reassurance. A pause after saying something like, 'You are worried that Marie is late. It sounds like you are feeling anxious?' gives the child permission to experience the feeling. A child who feels listened to will be more likely to share a worry such as, 'I'm afraid the bad man will get her.' The underlying fear is: 'I am afraid that a bad man may get me too.'

Parents miss a lot of great opportunities to educate children about relationships and sexuality when they fail to pick up what is behind children's indirect questions. If a child hears or sees something explicit on the media and the parent reacts by changing the programme, some children may pick up the wrong messages. They may think, 'My parents are not comfortable with this because it has to do with sex.' Saying something like, 'I feel uncomfortable watching that couple. It is rude to behave like that in public because people get embarrassed' is helpful. Older children might be ready for a more detailed explanation such as: 'I find this upsetting because when sex is used wrongly it not only hurts the people involved but it also hurts our whole society.'

TO SPEAK OR NOT

Experts differ about whether sexual scenes on the television affect children or not. It used to be thought that they went over children's heads. There are some studies which suggest that this is not so. When parents are prepared to discuss what children hear on the radio or see on the television it provides them with an opportunity to reassure them and pass on their values. Parents who say nothing on the assumption that a child does not understand what is happening may be making the right decision; on the other hand, if the child takes it all in he may be picking up undesirable attitudes to sexuality.

The storylines in most of the popular television soaps do not put forward the traditional values of sexual morality that most parents want their children to acquire. Given this, parents' understanding of how children are influenced by what they see and hear from media sources may help them decide if it is best to delay the sex education of the individual until puberty or not. Children in the same family can have such different personalities; the approach that suits one child may not work with another.

THE AMERICAN EXPERIENCE

Furthermore, parents are confused by contradictory advice from experts. Most countries have come to agree that lack of initiative in the home needs to be compensated by classroom instruction. In the United States New Jersey was the first state to require sex education for children in primary grades. When family life education was introduced into schools in 1980, almost 67 per cent of teenage births were to unmarried mothers. By the mid-1990s every public schoolchild in the state had an average of twenty-four hours of sex education a year. Most parents are aware of the content of the programme and a majority say that it is excellent or good. In spite of this, the teenage pregnancy rate has increased. It is not as high, however, as in some US cities where up to 85–90 per cent of teenage births are to unwed mothers, so people in favour of the programme in New Jersey feel the percentage might be even higher if sex education were not taught. Those against school-based programmes in America point to these increased figures to refute the idea that if teenagers are sexually active they should be privy to the information needed to avoid pregnancy and disease. The subject has become one for public comment: the Surgeon-General of the United States has said: 'Everyone in the world is opposed to sex outside of marriage and yet everybody does it' and President Clinton counsels sexual postponement and marriage before parenthood.

SEX EDUCATION IN BRITAIN AND IRELAND

In May 1994 the British Government directed that all schools revise their sex education programmes so that instruction takes place within a clear moral framework. Governors of primary schools have the authority to decide whether or not to have a sex education programme that goes beyond what is mandatory in the *National Curriculum Science Orders*. Secondary schools must offer a programme to all pupils, including information on sexually transmitted diseases. All schools are encouraged to consult with parents in order to devise an acceptable policy.

'Relationships and Sexuality Education' was made compulsory for all schoolchildren in Ireland a few months later. In July 1994, Niamh Bhreathnach, Minister for Education, announced that she was making the RSE programme mandatory in all schools. It took a further three years to train teachers to enable them to give the programme. As in Britain, provision was made for consultation with parents in producing a school policy. Parents were given the option of withdrawing a child from RSE classes.

The expected arguments were made by those in favour and those against the introduction of RSE. Here is an example of contradictory views from the *Irish Times* of 16 July 1994. Mr Peter Scully of Human Life International (an organisation that opposes school-based programmes) said sex education programmes introduced in other countries have failed utterly. 'In fact, their programmes lead to an enormous increase in teen promiscuity, teen pregnancy, abortion and rampant immorality in schools.' Senator Joe O'Toole, secretary of the Irish National Teachers Organisation took the opposite standpoint. He claimed that all children were entitled to sex education, that they were maturing much earlier, that child abuse was increasing, sex was more and more a feature of television programmes, and there was an annual increase in the number of teenage pregnancies and abortions.

In the same newspaper Anne Gill, chief executive of the Council for the Status of Women, said: 'Far too many young people continue to have inadequate information or misinformation, making it very difficult for them to make responsible and informed judgements.' A lack of such information, as we are well aware, can lead to major consequences for young people. It is no wonder that so many parents and teachers are confused about the effectiveness of school-based programmes.

EARLY QUESTIONS

There are some parents who still think that it is best to discourage a curious toddler from asking questions such as where babies come from. I suspect that most of us who are adults today came from families who passed on the belief that children are too young to be told about sex before puberty. The truth is that many adults are uncomfortable about their own lack of sex education. Thousands were left to discover the facts of sex for themselves. The whole of some people's sex education happened 'behind the bicycle shed at school' or in some equally unsuitable location. This is one reason why many adults do not have the vocabulary to talk about sex. Another is that children have their own jargon and many believe that they are better 'educated' about such practices as oral sex and alternative sexual orientations as homosexuality than their parents. Adults will not find the slang terms, 'blow job', 'rainbow kiss' or 'lick out' in any mainstream dictionary.

There are couples who have been married ten, twenty or more years who have never actually discussed their sexual desires, needs or wants with a spouse. It is understandable that a parent who finds it too embarrassing to discuss sexual matters with a spouse will be apprehensive about talking about them to a child. The result is that many parents who missed out on sex education are happy to pass on the responsibility to teachers who are professionally trained to do the job. One of the traditional misconceptions about delaying sex education was: 'If you don't tell them they won't find out.' The truth is that human sexuality and the feelings associated with it begin at birth and continue to the end of life. Some would say sex education begins even earlier, at conception.

It is now generally accepted that a child learns about sexuality in many hidden and subtle ways and that sex education has an emotional and spiritual dimension as well as a bodily one. Every parent gives continuing sex education whether intentionally or not. Parents give children a sense of the 'goodness' or 'badness' of body parts from the earliest days of life. If a parent is not comfortable about using the proper names for the genitals a child will assume that these body parts are embarrassing or taboo. Children sense how parents feel about the body and learn how they are expected to feel themselves.

Teaching a child about how the body works cannot be postponed until puberty. Parents need to be made more aware of how much silent sex education is given in the home by them at all ages. Between eighteen months and about three years a baby learns about sexual identity. Even before a child can talk he has begun to pick up his parents' values and attitudes. Three-year-olds understand that there are different social expectations for the sexes. By the age of four or five, children have have a sense of female/male stereotypes. Toddlers learn to give and receive affection from the way their parents show love and meet their own as well as their children's needs. A child's attitudes to intimacy are rooted in his very first experiences of it, which are usually with his mother and father.

PARENTAL AFFECTION

It is healthy for children to see their parents showing physical affection. When little ones see their parents kiss and cuddle affectionately they are likely to learn that physical affection is fun and enjoyable. They become comfortable with affectionate intimacy. The child learns a lot about himself as a sexual person from the way parents treat each other and from how they deal with sexual matters. Yet all families are not the same. Some people love to show affection with hugs and cuddles; others are not very comfortable with touching or physical intimacy. In fact lots of very warm, loving people learned not be demonstrative.

Around about seven years of age many boys warn their parents that they do not want to be kissed goodbye on the way into school. This does not happen so often with girls. It is important for parents to respect a child's wishes around this and to refrain from showing affection in public. However, it is equally important that the child is not totally deprived of affectionate touch. The macho seven-year-old at the school gate will still appreciate a goodnight hug or a cuddle when he is upset. We all need physical affection – adults as well as children. Not everyone is comfortable with hugs and embraces, so other gestures may be needed. Putting an arm around a shoulder, giving a pat on the back or touching a hand are also ways to be tactile. If you are a parent who is not comfortable about hugging your child it might be a good idea to find out where your discomfort comes from. One unfortunate effect of the publicity surrounding the reporting of child sexual abuse cases is that it has made some fathers afraid of being physically affectionate, particularly with daughters.

Children who miss out on the warmth of hugs and cuddles can feel deprived when they see other children enjoy them and they may think that they are not loved. In an ideal world a child could just ask to have his affectionate needs met. Sadly most children are never taught to communicate honestly about their wants and needs. If parents are so intent on keeping children innocent that sex is a taboo subject in the home the child may learn to equate touch with sex. Children who do not get timely information often feel guilty about their natural sexual curiosity.

LEARNING ABOUT SEXUAL STEREOTYPES

Sex education begins from the first days of a baby's life. Mum and Dad are the primary educators of children even when issues about relationships and sexuality are never mentioned by them. The child learns what it means to be a girl or boy by copying the actions of others of the same sex. For example, girls imitate their mothers and other female role models. Boys learn how men are expected to behave by watching their fathers and other men. In this way children learn that girls are supposed to do certain things and boys do different things. The girl senses: 'I'm a girl because I don't do boy things.'

Between the ages of three and six, children begin to

learn how women and men in our society are expected to behave simply by watching how Mum and Dad treat each other. If Mum and Dad respect each other and treat each other as equals the child has wonderful role models. If a couple have problems in their relationship the child quickly senses that something is wrong. Some children blame themselves. They think: if I was good this would not happen. A child's security is highly dependent on the quality of the relationship between the parents. When Mum and Dad have a happy, fulfilled sex life the child senses the warmth of their relationship and learns to feel good about his body.

What parents unconsciously teach a child about sex and relationships is deeply influenced by their own childhood experiences. If the child's grandparents were not comfortable about sexual matters it is almost certain that the parents learned to feel uncomfortable too. Though many people may say, 'No one ever told me about any of these things and it never did me a bit of harm', I am not convinced. When a parent fails to give guidance the child is always left unsupported and unsure.

APPRECIATING SEXUALITY AS A GIFT
Virginia Satir, the family therapist, has written:

If you had seen as much pain as I have that clearly resulted from inhuman and repressive attitudes about sex, you would turn yourself inside out immediately to change your whole attitude to one of open acceptance, pride, enjoyment and appreciation of the spirituality of sex. Instead, I have found

that most families employ the rule, 'Don't enjoy sex
- yours or anyone else's - in any form.'

She also says that unless we openly understand, value,
and enjoy our sexual side as well as that of the opposite
sex, we are literally paving the way for serious personal
pain. If a parent is free to enjoy and appreciate her God-
given gift of sexuality she will model that freedom for
children. If that freedom is lacking it suggests that the
parent needs to explore her own sexuality to come to a
more positive understanding. It is unfortunate that the
desire to protect a child's innocence may be the biggest
obstacle to ensuring that children are given relationships
and sexuality education that is relevant to their family
situation and life experiences.

2

TODDLERS

It is widely accepted that children of parents who have a positive and open attitude to sex are more likely to grow up with a well-adjusted attitude to sexual matters. The most significant factor in how we relate to other people emotionally and sexually is the influence of our family of origin. The meaning of the word 'family' has changed. It no longer describes only the traditional family where Mum and Dad are married to each other and have children. A lot of children live in less traditional family units. Some belong to single-parent families because their mothers have never been married or their parents have separated. Others live with two parents who cohabit. A smaller number live in blended families where parents bring together children from other relationships to live as a new family.

It is important for a parent to ensure that when a child begins school (or even pre-school) that he is not made feel that his family situation is unacceptable. Most teachers are aware of how sensitive parents are about how the word 'family' is used. They know that not every child is living with married parents. It would be presumptuous to assume that all single-parent families are made up of a mother and offspring; it is rarer for the father to become the sole parent but it does happen.

There is no evidence to show that married couples make better parents, but there *is* evidence to indicate that couples who are experiencing family conflict are less effective as parents and often neglect the needs of children. Some children in single-parent families are deprived of role models for adult relationships because they do not have the opportunity to observe a continuing couple-relationship. Traditional families can also offer children poor and even dysfunctional models. For example, a father who is so busy with work or a hobby that he fails to spend time with his family is effectively an absent spouse and parent. He is a poor role model for a boy.

Any parent who understands how to show love and respect for a child helps him grow into a well-adjusted person. It is true that children brought up by affectionate married parents are more likely to achieve love and stability in their adult relationships. It is equally true that married parents who are constantly bickering and finding fault rear children with a negative model of family relationships.

MISSING THE FATHER
Children learn an enormous amount about relationships before they begin school. How Dad behaves towards Mum sets an example for how the son will treat his girlfriend or wife later on. If Dad is not around because of separation

or desertion or an unmarried pregnancy, the family is incomplete. If Mum is parenting on her own she must be very careful not to let her child get distorted ideas about how women and men relate.

If she resents being on her own and talks about Dad in a disapproving way there is a danger that the child may internalise the negative message and feel that males are bad. The message that it is not good to be male has a damaging effect. A boy is also in danger of being fussed over by Mum and becoming a 'Mammy's boy'. Some lads respond to their father's absence by taking on the role of mother's little protector. Later in life they remain tied to Mum and fail to act on their own heterosexual interest. Boys living with Mum in lone-parent families may learn to perceive women as dominant, and if Mum takes control her young daughter may believe that this is how women should be: dominant, controlling and independent of men.

THE NEED FOR LOVE AND SECURITY

I am not for a moment suggesting that a child has to live with two happily married parents in order to be able to sustain a long-term stable relationship as an adult. Not alone is that untrue but it ignores the reality of life in the modern world. What I am saying is that it is vital for parents to understand a child's needs for love and security. When a child knows that he is cherished, the sense of being loved and accepted builds up trust and self-esteem. These qualities are vitally important in learning to give and receive love as a child, and later on as an adult.

FAMILY CONFLICT

There are no perfect families. Every couple experiences relationship problems from time to time. Children disobey a parent who has had a bad day; tempers flare and angry words get shouted. Some conflict is a part of normal family life. Most couples get over the upset. Some apologise and ask to be forgiven; others do not.

When a couple has more serious problems children know about it even when the parents try to hide what is happening. It helps if a mother can be frank and explain: 'I was angry with your Dad for getting drunk last night. He has an illness called alcoholism and this helps me to forgive him.' When a parent is honest and shares how she feels in this way the child is not only reassured but actually learns about love, respect and forgiveness. This kind of frankness can do a lot to build self-esteem, improve communication and minimise the emotional hurt suffered by a child.

QUESTIONS

When a child enjoys good communication with a parent he feels loved and secure. He develops a good sense of his own self-worth. This self-esteem is a vital part of the emotional and sexual development of every child. There are no genes to carry feelings of self-worth; these are learned from parents and other family members. When a child feels worthwhile he has the confidence to ask questions and expect to get answers. It is here that sex education has its most appropriate opportunity but the opportunity can be missed if the parent does not or cannot answer, either through feelings of shame or embarrassment or uncertainty of approach.

There is no set formula for answering a question like, 'Why doesn't she have a daddy?' or 'Why are you a lone parent?' If a parent ignores the question or admonishes the child for asking, this shows disapproval. He just does not understand why. If the query relates to sexual matters such as body parts or babies, the child may get negative messages about sexuality. The result is that some children may assume that parents frown on sexual curiosity. This is not necessarily true. One reason that many parents hesitate to reply is that they are nervous of damaging the child's innocence. Most experts suggest that a child feels more secure when a parent is prepared to be open and frank.

INSTANT INFORMATION?

It is not always essential to give the information immediately. If the parent is not sure what to say, she should give herself time. It is quite proper to tell a child: 'I need to think about that. I will talk to you when you are going to bed', or whatever time is suitable. I cannot put too much stress on how important it is to stick to the arrangement and not let the child down. Let me reassure any parent who has avoided answering such questions not to be worried. Information alone will not guarantee a healthy attitude to sex. Studies have shown that some children who had sex education from a parent, attended programmes in school and had access to appropriate books, still did not have a healthy attitude to sexuality as adults. The explanation for this was that their family life was unhappy. Either their parents had a miserable relationship or the child did not feel loved. Quite often both situations went together.

In Victorian times many girls had the opposite experience. They remained ignorant about sexual intercourse until they got married. Those whose parents had a sound relationship were not damaged by the experience. They managed to adjust quickly and they learned to enjoy sex every bit as much as their more knowledgeable sisters do today.

It is clear that detailed information about the physical aspects of sexuality is not the most important aspect of relationship education. Although such information is necessary, it is pointless for a parent to try to give it if she senses that the child feels too embarrassed to listen. The crucially important factor is the influence on the child of the parents' relationship with each other and with the child.

UNREASONABLE EXPECTATIONS

The most influential theories about the kind of sex education children need came from the work of Sigmund Freud. He recognised that there was a connection between various neuroses and the guilty, frightening ideas some children acquire about sex in early childhood. Many early educators assumed sexual disturbances were caused when children did not have the facts of life explained to them correctly. Freud believed that with proper instruction it should be possible to prevent most adults from developing sexual neuroses. The kind of problems that he felt could be alleviated included frigidity in women, impotence in men, perversions, homosexuality and obsessive and compulsive neuroses.

Later research showed he was too optimistic. The more likely causes of neuroses lay in the disturbed feelings of a child towards a parent or parents. For example, an abnormally close and possessive relationship between a child and a parent is now thought to create neurotic symptoms. Experience has also shown that giving children the facts about sex did not banish neuroses or do away with aberrant sexuality in adults.

HIDDEN SEX EDUCATION

Parents are constantly teaching children about sexuality, whether they are aware of it or not. The language they use to describe the genitals influences a child about his attitude to these body parts. A lot of young boys think that a girl was meant to have a penis and worry if she lost it accidentally. Little girls may think along similar lines as well. Some boys worry that they might lose their penis and wonder if that would turn them into a girl. They may also worry about penis size, especially if they have caught a glimpse of Dad's penis in a toilet or bathroom. This anxiety is sometimes carried into adulthood. Many grown men have worries about the size of their member. The current belief is that they might not have such anxiety if their fathers had reassured them early enough. The suggestion is that a father might say something like, 'Look at my feet. Now they are bigger than yours. As you grow your feet will grow bigger and so will the rest of your body. When you grow up your penis will get bigger too.'

Small girls may need reassurance too. They need to be told very clearly that girls are not meant to have a penis because they are made differently from boys. If the question is asked it provides a good opportunity to explain that girls and boys have different sexual equipment; girls have a vulva, boys have a penis. It also gives a parent the chance to teach some basic hygiene: a little girl should wipe from front to back after going to the toilet. It is important also to be sensitive to the fact that some small girls incorrectly associate their genitals with going to the toilet and may consider the area between the legs to be 'dirty'.

Where do babies come from?

Around three or four years of age a child is likely to ask questions about babies and where they come from. Up until the very recent past it was common to avoid telling very young children about pregnancy. We now know that misguided attempts to keep children innocent only confused them. A child as young as three is likely to have an idea of where the baby grows. Toddlers pick up a surprising amount of information from television and from the bits of conversation they overhear. If Mum or a close friend or family member is pregnant, the child will notice her growing bigger. If Mum lies or fails to explain properly, the child may worry.

The first questions children ask usually require only simple answers. It is natural that a child who understands that a baby grows in a special place called the womb will want to know how did the baby get in and how does it come out. There is no need to overreact when a toddler asks these questions. He is probably not looking for information about intercourse but showing natural curiosity.

Small children know that when they eat something it goes into their stomach. They want to check if the baby got into the womb from something the mother ate. A simple explanation like, 'The baby grows from a tiny seed that was there all the time' will usually keep him happy.

Experts disagree on whether to explain to toddlers about the father's part in the process. Some think that little boys benefit from knowing that the father has an important part to play in making babies. Others feel that it may be upsetting to give a child an exact picture of intercourse. The parent is the best person to decide what is right for a particular child. I am a great believer in giving a child a little information to satisfy his curiosity. Then I ask, 'Does that answer your question?' The child will tell you soon enough if he needs more information.

Little children do not want too many facts. Explain things very simply and be wary of giving more information than the child needs. A simple answer to 'Will a baby grow in my tummy?' is 'No. God (or Mother Nature) doesn't give babies to little girls. Grown-ups get a baby when a little seed, called the ovum, in the woman's body meets a sperm, a little seed from the man's body.' If that seems sufficient leave more detail to another occasion. If you are asked how the baby comes out of the mother's body say something like, 'When the baby is ready to be born he comes into the world through a special opening between the mummy's legs.' If more information is wanted you could expand a little: 'The baby grows in the womb which is like a little room in the mother's body. When she is ready she comes into the world through the birth canal – that is like a little corridor out of the womb into the world.' You may like to explain that it is called the vagina or you may feel that this is unnecessary.

It is well for parents to realise that even when they give young children clear and simple answers to their questions the children forget or get mixed up about what they have been told. If you are a parent of a young child be prepared to correct wrong information. You will have to repeat what you have told them more than once. When the child comes to puberty a wise parent assumes they have forgotten whatever answers they got to their earlier questions and explains everything again.

No questions?

Some toddlers ask a lot of questions and some ask none. Most experts agree that children are naturally curious about the differences between women's and men's bodies, but that is where the agreement ends. There are different explanations for the fact that certain children do not have queries. Some believe children are so upset when they notice that men and women are made differently that they do not care to enquire about why this is. Others conclude that the child must have asked a question that embarrassed the parent and so learned that the parent disapproved of questions on these topics. It is thought that if a child has received a negative response he will feel that it is not good to ask certain kinds of questions.

Confusion

Sex education involves far more than simply answering questions and giving accurate information. As we have seen, even when a parent is very careful to explain matters to a child there is no guarantee that the child will remember accurately. Young children seldom fully understand what they are told. Some of them use their imaginations, embroider the facts and arrive at conclusions of their own. When a child comes out with something outrageous a parent often assumes the child is getting wrong information from other children. This is not always the case. Lots of children dream up new facts themselves.

A playgroup leader once overheard five-year-old Sarah explain to four-year-old Emma how her new baby sister was born. 'The baby grew and grew and grew inside my Mum's tummy. Then my Daddy brought her to the hospital because the baby wanted to come out. Then my Mum's belly button popped out. The baby jumped out. My Mum put her belly button back in and she called my sister Johanna.'

The information a parent gives is not nearly as important as the fact that the discussion is taking place. A young child feels secure when he enjoys good communication with parents who are open and frank. A parent who is relaxed enough to talk about sexual issues is generally comfortable with her own sexuality. If a parent makes the effort to talk about the facts of sex to a toddler he learns that it is all right to discuss these issues. He will then feel free to ask questions when he is older. Such is the ideal. In the next chapter we will see that the practice does not always bear this out.

3

PUBERTY

NATURAL CURIOSITY

It is sad that many parents worry about telling children the facts of life. The fear of burdening children with information that might destroy their innocence is still very prevalent. Yet young people often successfully conceal from parents and teachers that they are anything but innocent. Most have an enormous amount of sexual information. By eleven or twelve years of age lots of girls and some boys will have reached puberty. Although most are well-versed in the mechanics of human reproduction, few accept traditional standards of sexual morality. Good relationship and sexuality education involves non-judgemental listening on the part of parent, teacher or counsellor. Students need help to put the sexual information they have within a moral and spiritual framework. I suspect that the majority of adults also need to be educated about the spirituality of sexuality. The acceptance of oneself as a spiritual being is just as important to the rounded development of the person as the acceptance of one's sexuality.

It is clear that young people are physically ready for sex before they are emotionally ready for loving relationships. Hormonal activity begins this process of readiness and children as young as ten or eleven years of age often become intensely if secretly interested in sexuality. They sense, too, that parents would disapprove if they knew of this preoccupation and so it is nurtured as an excitingly forbidden interest. The heightened awareness of sexuality both girls and boys experience at puberty makes them incredibly curious about anything to do with the body and the opposite sex. They are fascinated by the thought of women and men having sex. They want to know what it feels like. They are captivated by the idea of who does what to whom and how long it takes to 'do it'. Television programmes, magazines and videos give them more answers than adults do.

ADOLESCENTS' ROLE MODELS

Youngsters learn a little about what is appropriate sexual behaviour from what they are told by adults; they learn an enormous amount from watching how couples behave on media presentations. They are particularly influenced by how they see adolescents acting on television. Some actually practise how to be like their idols. They imitate them in dress, speech and behaviour. It is important for parents who want to give sex education at puberty to be sensitive to what young people learn from their favourite actors and their peers.

Girls, as a rule, reach puberty a year or two earlier than boys. It is no longer rare for a ten-year-old girl to get her periods. Girls who mature early and boys who mature late are the ones who have the most difficult time during adolescence. The earlier a girl matures the earlier her first sexual experience is likely to be. Girls and boys who have friends who have developed before them need to be constantly reassured. They should be told: 'You will reach puberty at the right time for you.' Parents should be aware that even before the earliest physical signs of puberty appear, children experience vague bodily sensations and emotional stirrings related to their changing internal chemistry. The age at which bodily changes begin can range from between approximately ten to fourteen for a girl and a year or two later for a boy. This is a time of rapid physical development, when sexual reproduction first becomes possible. Early or late development in a child is influenced by such factors as heredity, nutrition and general health. I use the word *puberty* when writing about the many physical changes that occur during the pre-teen and teenage years and intend the term *adolescent* to include pre-teens who have reached puberty as well as those in their teenage years.

BEGINNING

There is no doubt that sex education is as emotive an issue today as it ever was. Some parents set out to educate a child from birth and are comfortable dealing frankly with relationships as well as sexuality education. Others who perhaps did not have a good sex education themselves, would prefer if a teacher, counsellor or nurse would do it for them. Some parents like to read a book with a child, and some leave the book in the child's room and say nothing. Who is to say which approach is best?

One thing can be said with certainty. Children need a holistic approach to sexuality that educates them about the body, mind and spirit. They need to understand that being sexual affects one physically, emotionally and spiritually.

It is important to remember that no two children, even identical twins, are exactly alike. Within the same family there are children with totally different personalities. The approach that works with a shy, introverted child may be a total disaster with a more extrovert one. As well, many parents have found that having waited to talk to a child about the facts of life until around the time of puberty, and having prepared themselves to initiate the discussion, they are greeted with: 'I know all that already.' It is not uncommon for a parent to feel upset and blame herself when this occurs: 'I must have picked the wrong time', or 'If only I had done it differently', or 'I should have started when he was younger.' There is little point in such recrimination. If you are a parent who has had this experience, accept that there is no right time. If your child is not willing to cooperate with you, every time is the wrong time.

One reason for this may be that the child learned earlier in his life not to ask questions. This probably happened when he first asked questions about babies and his parents avoided answering. My eldest daughter was one of these. I started out as a protective parent who did not answer questions frankly. I was better informed and more able to answer questions with my second daughter. By the time the two younger girls came along I had totally changed my approach. I did everything that the experts recommended. Sensitive to the theory that sex education begins from the first days of a child's life, I could not have started younger. I took the initiative. I invited questions and gave detailed answers. It made not one bit of difference once they reached puberty. They confided in their peers and not in me.

Other parents tell me they have had similar experiences. I meet hundreds of parents every year who answer every question a child thinks to ask. They are more than willing to discuss sexual issues with a daughter or son but are never given the opportunity. Occasionally I meet parents who have had a different experience. They have given their children informative books to read because they could not bring themselves to discuss sex. The children have read the books and amazed the parents by chatting comfortably about the contents afterwards. The children's naturalness has helped the parents to feel more comfortable too.

SEX AND SPIRITUALITY

No one can tell you how a child will react to a talk about the birds and bees. Nor can anyone tell you exactly what to say to your own child. They can only make suggestions that have worked for other people. There is no guarantee that these will work with your offspring. The effort must, however, be made; otherwise the child will look elsewhere for the information and from sources that do not consider moral or spiritual aspects. Parents or teachers giving sex education need to help young people understand how easy it is to confuse sexual arousal with love. The media teach them to have an appreciation of erotic love but seldom bring out the sacredness of such love. In the past poor religious teaching taught people to equate sexual pleasure with sin and there are people today who still carry a residue of the terrible damage that such teaching has done. Many genuinely believe that religion is opposed to sex. Priests and ministers seldom take the opportunity to contradict this view and preach about a more positive appreciation of the sacredness of bodily intimacy.

Young people need to be taught that there should be no shame about the proper utilisation of sexuality. God made us female and male. We were created as sexual people. When our body responds in a sexual way we should feel happy and celebrate that we are sensual people. Sexual feelings and desires are normal and natural and not something one should feel guilty about. Young people are not made sufficiently aware that the Christian churches value sexuality. This may be because their parents are unaware of it too. Many adults may be surprised to learn that there are many different theologies of sexuality, not just one. Some are so positive about sex that they use sexual union as a symbol for spiritual union.

HEART TO HEART
There is no magic formula for giving sex education at puberty. I can almost guarantee failure for any parent planning a face-to-face chat. They just do not work, because they are terribly intimidating for a child. A far better way to talk is when you are side-by-side, perhaps when you are out walking. Some experienced parents recommend the time when you are washing dishes to-gether. One woman told me that a great time to talk to a

child is when you are washing his hair. He can say, 'I know all that already', but he is in no position to run away.

Around puberty and the early stages of adolescence children seldom cooperate in a heart-to-heart discussion with parents. Other people's children freely talk to me about everything. When my own daughters were going through the early stages of puberty they censored what I was allowed to hear. When they were finished that stage we had some great discussions sharing reminiscences. I took great pleasure in complimenting one daughter several years after she impressed me with a very quick-thinking recovery. One evening the family were sitting down to dinner and the two older girls were having one of those giggly conversations that are so common with adolescents. We heard the word 'masturbation'. 'What did I hear you say?' my spouse enquired. Quick as a flash came the reply, 'We are talking about mastication.'

My daughters reacted just like thousands of other adolescents who refuse to discuss sexual issues with adults. Youngsters project their own discomfort on to their parents. They like to think they are protecting them from embarrassment but what they are doing is protecting themselves. They have the good sense to know their parents would be appalled by the crude and vulgar information they get from magazines and books, and from their peers. So they protect them. They hide their salacious interest in matters sexual from adults who would find it shocking. They wait until they are in the company of their peers to huddle in little groups to discuss the latest 'sca'. They talk about what is happening on their favourite television programmes. Girls often bring teenage magazines to school to share their views on the problem pages.

MYTHS

A parent can do very little to protect young people from the influence of the peer group and what I call 'street education'. The one suggestion I can offer is to listen sensitively to the information your child already has. The kind of sexual information children from as young as ten years of age share with their peers can be quite shocking. Before I started teaching a relationship and sexuality education programme in schools I had no suspicion that children were so knowledgeable about some aspects of sexuality and so ignorant of others. I discovered that all the old myths about sex that I had been told when I was growing up were still doing the rounds: a girl cannot get pregnant if she has sex standing up; it is safe to have sex during a period; it is impossible to become pregnant the first time one has sex. They also believe the oldest story of all, that he will withdraw before ejaculation and she cannot become pregnant. Isn't it frightening to think that any young couple would have sex believing those tall tales? Unless these myths are exposed as lies, ill-informed young people will remain vulnerable and at risk.

FIRST INTIMACY

What makes sexual ignorance even more frightening is that children are reaching puberty sooner than in previous generations. The earlier a girl matures the earlier her first sexual experience is likely to be. The first contact for most young couples today is French kissing, usually on the dance floor at a disco. For some boys it happens before they have even reached puberty. I have no doubt that parents and teachers need to be more aware of the young age at which children begin kissing intimately. I suspect that many parents protect themselves from this unacceptable truth. I know I did. I told myself: 'It could happen with some children but certainly not with mine.' The truth is it happens with all adolescents – sooner rather than later.

Girls usually mature earlier than boys and they are more often the initiators of intimate kissing. Too many parents refrain from discussing kissing with younger children from the best of motives; they are afraid of putting ideas into their child's head and worry that the mention of it will encourage a precocious interest in intimacy. There is, however, no evidence to show that this is true. On the contrary, there is a lot of evidence to show that children are already interested in these matters, and research shows that those whose parents discuss sexuality with them are more likely to delay intimate activity.

When girls and boys are 'getting off' they are being sexual in a way that can lead to a desire for intimate touching. French kissing, 'shifting' or 'meeting' has more to do with acting grown-up than it has to do with showing affection. Primary school children will tell you, 'You have to do it if you get up for a slow dance', and if you ask why, you will be told, 'Because everybody does it.' Parents must wake up to the fact that the old romantic preliminaries like hand-holding have been rejected in favour of intimate kissing, which is casually accepted as the norm. There is a generally held belief that children who have good self-esteem and self-confidence are more likely to remain aloof from these activities. I am not so sure that this is true. I believe that some early-maturing, confident girls exercise their freedom to show they are interested in boys.

This creates its own problems for boys, especially those who are late developers. It is not macho in our society for a lad who is asked out by a girl to turn her down. As a typical illustration of what happens, let us consider a group of girls who are standing a little distance away from a crowd of lads. One of the girls fancies a particular boy. She tells her friends, and perhaps one, but more usually two or three, offer to go across and ask the boy if he will go out with her. When this happens he may feel trapped. He is lucky if he is with a group who are not yet interested in girls. He can refuse. If he admits to having an interest in girls he is caught. If she is a good-looking, attractive girl his mates will expect him to say yes. The only acceptable reason for refusal is having a girlfriend already.

WORRIES ABOUT SEXUAL ORIENTATION

It is easy to imagine how a lad who has not yet reached puberty must feel when he is coerced into dating before he is ready. There is bound to be regret that she is not the girl he might have wanted to choose, and anger against all concerned, including himself. Usually boys do not have the insight to recognise or admit that they are reacting to peer pressure. They are reluctant to acknowledge that they feel trapped. A boy in our society who rejects a girl who comes on to him is likely to be teased.

Some schoolboys pretend they are interested in girls because they risk being labelled gay if they do not. No boy wants to risk making a fool of himself among his friends.

It is dreadful to think that boys worry about their sexual orientation at such a young age. Good sex education should give them the reassurance they need to delay dating. I meet teenage boys each year who are the 'victims' of being set up with a girl. 'What is the worst thing that would happen if you were honest and said how you feel?' I sometimes ask lads who come to me privately to talk about these kinds of situations. 'I couldn't tell her. She'd tell her friends and everybody would laugh at me. They'd say I was gay.'

SEXUAL PRESSURE

It is clear that a boy who agrees to go with a girl because of peer pressure is allowing himself to be treated as a sex object. Equally, a girl who makes out with a boy because she is afraid of being labelled frigid is responding to sexual pressure. Girls and boys who intimately kiss every person they partner at a disco are not showing love. They are just using others for sexual thrills – or again responding to pressure. Surely this is not the introduction to relationships with the other sex that a caring parent would want for a child? The peer group acceptance of intimately kissing someone who is attractive *in the absence of a loving relationship* must be challenged.

One way to help young people deal with sexual pressure is to share your concern with them. A good way to do this is to encourage them to think about how they would react in various situations. If a parent constantly says no to requests without explaining the reasons, children become angry and resentful. I often ask young people who complain about unreasonable parents to tell me what essays and parents have in common. When I tell them the answer is: 'Who? What? When? Where? How? Why?' I look on a sea of blank faces. Then I explain that the checklist for an essay is exactly the same as the checklist successful teenagers use to be allowed out.

I explain why it is important to make an effort to keep parents well informed. If adolescents can show they are trustworthy by telling their parents their intentions they are showing maturity. This may persuade parents to give them greater freedom or it may not. I tell them that parents have the right to know:

- who you plan to meet
- what you plan to do
- where you are going
- when you will be home
- how you plan to get there and back and if you have the money to pay
- why you choose to spend your time in that way

The issues that worry most parents are smoking, drinking, unsuitable friends and illegal drugs. When young people understand why parents are worried it can make it easier for them to accept refusals when they are not allowed the same freedom as their friends. Good communication is the secret of happy relationships.

If your twelve-year-old wishes to go out with friends do not make an immediate decision. Ask questions. Look for information. Many parents want to express to their children their concerns about pre-teen French kissing. If you feel worried, spell out why you are anxious. Explain exactly what it is that concerns you. Give girls and boys factual information about how common it is for youngsters their age to find themselves in situations that they cannot handle. You could say to a son: 'I'm worried knowing that girls come on to boys nowadays that a sexy girl might proposition you'; and to a daughter: 'I trust you but I am worried about older boys who take advantage of younger girls.' Ask them to tell you how they would handle such situations. 'Tell me what you would do if you got up to dance with someone who immediately began kissing you intimately. At your age I would have been tongue-tied. I don't mean that as a joke although it would be difficult to talk with two tongues in your mouth.' This may sound crude but it is specific. It makes your concern clear and starts the adolescent son or daughter thinking.

Most young people have very confused feelings about sexual advances from the other sex. As one very aware young girl commented on intimate kissing: 'I like it and I don't like it. At first you feel sexy and that feels good.' She went on to explain that she liked when a boy held her very close. It is important for parents to understand how important affectionate intimacy is for young people. She continued: 'I felt all grown-up. I felt like a desirable woman. Then when he forced his tongue into my mouth I didn't like that. I felt funny, like I should be enjoying it or something and I wasn't. It felt cold and wet – but I let him.' This intelligent young girl tried out grown-up behaviour and had mixed feelings. Being close to a boy felt good but she was disappointed that the kissing was not enjoyable. Until we discussed the matter she did not realise that she could tell him that although she liked dancing close she didn't like that kind of kissing.

NEGATIVE REINFORCEMENT

I suspect that the majority of parents explain the facts of sex in order to prevent teenage pregnancies and AIDS. Some warn against the serious dangers of other sexually transmitted diseases. This kind of preventive teaching reinforces negative messages. I believe that relationships education would be more effective if parents set out to give a positive understanding of what it means to relate as a sexual person; yet this may be asking too much as many parents do not have a positive appreciation of their own sexuality.

Young people are often unfairly accused of lacking a proper attitude to sexual values. They openly admit that they do not see any value in remaining a virgin until marriage. This is hardly surprising. What are looked on as good old-fashioned values were usually motivated by fear of pregnancy rather than by virtue. That fear was banished by contraception. Fertility control became the key that opened the shackles to a new sexual freedom.

Some parents have unreasonably high expectations of school-based sex education programmes. They imagine that teachers will meet all the needs of students at every stage of their development. Some even assume that teachers will inculcate a positive attitude to sexual abstinence. These RSE programmes cannot achieve miracles; teachers can only build on the foundations already laid by parents, who are the primary educators of children. Many, whether they are aware of it or not, teach the child to have a positive or negative attitude to sexuality. If a pupil feels that sex is dirty, sinful or shameful, the teacher will find it difficult to counter that attitude.

It is becoming clear that a different approach to sex education is needed in the permissive Western world. The horrifying revelations of child sex-abuse cases from every part of the globe has alerted governments to the necessity of educating young people to protect themselves from sexual pressure and abuse. The widespread confusion between physical intimacy and sexual taboos will not be dissipated by school-based programmes alone. Many parents admit that they need to be sexually re-educated themselves. Most educators recognise the vitally important role every parent plays in the child's education about sex and relationships. Few publicly acknowledge the negative parental influences of dysfunctional families.

It cannot be repeated too often that adolescents have learned expectations of relationships. They are likely to model their behaviour with the opposite sex on how they have observed their parents acting towards each other. Their expectations of affective sexuality – receiving and giving love – are deeply influenced by how parents show love. This relationship education is the foundation on which are built the attitudes of adolescents, and it colours the nature of their romances.

4

ADOLESCENCE

CHANGING ATTITUDES TO SEX

Adolescents need to discover that becoming good friends
with the other sex is the first step to building healthy
intimacy in a relationship. They need to be made aware
of how important it is to meet one's affective relationship
needs. It is natural for teenagers to want to experiment
sexually and therefore it is vital that they be made aware
that having sex too soon tends to blur the distinction
between lust and intimacy needs. 'Safe sex' advertisements, which are meant to convince people that it is
irresponsible to have pre-marital sex without using a
condom, have had their message perverted; they are taken
to mean that pre-marital sex in young people is perfectly
all right as long as a condom is used. These advertisements are specifically meant to prevent the spread of
sexually transmitted diseases (STDs) and are deliberately
worded so as to make no moral statement. Inevitably they
fail to convey the message that making love is a life-
changing decision. It is also unfortunate that recent sexual
scandals have somewhat impugned the authority of

religious teaching in controlling sexual behaviour.

We have seen that when parents and adolescents communicate well, young people are more likely to delay sexual activity. Good communication is lacking when young people are told what they should or should not do. Imposing standards of behaviour simply does not work. Parents who disapprove of pre-marital sex can advise against it. They can forbid it but they can do absolutely nothing to stop it. They are not going to be around when it happens.

If a girl is happy to French-kiss a boy she has just met on the dance floor it should come as no surprise that intimate touching will follow on fairly quickly. In early adolescence girls and boys fall in and out of love frequently. First love is usually infatuation and is short-lived. Parents may be inclined to underestimate the intensity of feelings that their son or daughter will experience in these early romances. It is not unusual for eleven and twelve-year-olds to become sexually aroused and experience the excitement and joys of first passion. Those of us who are parents of adolescents today are faced with problems and difficulties that are new and were not faced by our parents or previous generations. If we believe newspaper reports, we must accept that girls and boys are sexually active from a very early age.

Psychologist Maureen Gaffney reports research findings that: 'Girls who date early, by the age of fourteen, are likely to have sexual intercourse before they leave second-level education, are less likely to use contraception and are more likely to become pregnant.' As puberty approaches it is only natural that children become intensely curious about what sexual experience is like, and ideally they should talk to their parents. The reality is that few parents encourage them and many never talk to their children about sex. Some feel they have done their duty by explaining bodily changes and human reproduction but this kind of mechanical information alone will not motivate young people to delay sexual activity, nor will it have much effect in changing their attitudes or behaviour.

FINDING A LANGUAGE

Unquestionably there is a lot of pressure on adolescents to allow intimate touching once a relationship develops. Most children have been sexualised by the media by the time they reach puberty, and in general, television programmes and videos ignore the values of sexual morality that were taken for granted in our society until very recently. Many pre-teens assume that French kissing outside of a loving relationship is acceptable because 'Everybody does it.' It is important for parents to challenge them to consider this widely held assumption: 'If everybody does something does that make it OK for you to do it? Is intimate kissing in the absence of a loving relationship acceptable?'

Some adolescents feel protected from sexual pressure when they engage in kissing at a disco. It is seen as harmless because nobody gets hurt. I am not sure that this is true. Intimate kissing frequently gives rise to resentful feelings that one allowed oneself to be used. It is never acceptable to use others for sexy thrills. Yet most parents fail to challenge young people who hold these ideas. Adolescents assume, and who could blame them, that adult silence means consent. A surprising number of young people argue that there is nothing harmful in treating others as sexual objects provided both parties consent. This thinking has long-term consequences for individuals and for society.

The earlier young people begin to kiss the sooner they move on to petting and other forms of sexual intimacy. They are likely to have sexual intercourse as the next step in the progression. These are matters that a concerned parent needs to discuss with her adolescent children. The conversation requires delicate handling because the intimacy needs of girls and boys are so very different. Talking about what is appropriate behaviour for dating couples may involve language problems too. The words some young people use may be incomprehensible to adults. They are not to be found in the conventional dictionary. I suspect that most parents would not feel comfortable using teenage terminology. Yet equally they are wisely reluctant to use language that sounds too clinical and cold.

For example, a girl may describe a handsome-looking fellow as a 'ride', a 'screw', or a 'lash'. Such terms that seem harmless to adolescents are enough to put parents into a blind panic about what their offspring is doing. The experience of a mother – let us call her Mary Smith – is typical of what can happen. She found a note in her daughter Sarah's room and it upset her. The note read: 'Hi Sarah, I'm glad you think Dave's a ride. I think he is really cool. I'll phone you tonight. C.' If she confronted Sarah about the note she would have to admit that she had been snooping. If she let the matter go, her daughter might come home pregnant. She could think of two of Sarah's classmates whose names started with 'C'. She must have been out last night when 'C' rang. She had no idea who Dave was or what age he was. She was sick at the prospect. Her Sarah said, 'Dave's a ride.' How did she know? Had she been with him? She was too young to have sex – or was she? The words kept echoing in her head. 'Dave's a ride.' Finally Mary could stand it no longer. She needed to talk to someone but had a problem deciding in whom to confide.

She thought about the principal of Sarah's school and immediately dismissed the idea. She did not want to involve the school. She knew Catherine's mother but maybe the C was not for Catherine. It could be Carol. She did not have a telephone number for either of them. If she rang Sarah's father he would lose the cool altogether. Eventually after a good deal of soul-searching she decided to telephone her sister-in-law Jennifer, who had three older teenagers. Perhaps she could advise her as to what she should do. She knew that what she had to say would be respected and treated in confidence. Jennifer laughed when Mary told her the problem. Yes, she had heard one of her girls say something similar. She had exactly the same reaction as Mary before she found out what it meant. 'A ride is not what you think; it just means that Dave is a good-looking boy.'

CRUDE AND VULGAR LANGUAGE

Many parents find themselves in Mary's situation. They come across crude notes or overhear vulgar pieces of conversations and are not sure how to deal with them. Is it best to address the issue or ignore it and say nothing? There is no doubt that girls and boys are interested in talking about sex from about ten or eleven years of age. They use their own jargon which includes lots of crude and vulgar expressions. Many parents feel they need to know the meaning and connotations of these slang terms before they can challenge disrespectful attitudes to sexuality.

I think it is important to address such issues whenever they arise. Adolescents are incredibly indiscreet when they are on the telephone or when they are watching television or chatting among themselves in the back of a car. It is perfectly in order for a parent who overhears crude remarks or vulgar language to say something like, 'I could not help but overhear you say Dave is a ride', or whatever the remark was. 'I'm not sure that I understand what that means.' Tell them how you feel about crude language. 'I find that kind of language offensive', or 'I feel disappointed to hear you talk about boys (or girls) in that hurtful way.' Decide what it is you object to and then say whatever you feel you need to say.

This is the most effective way of sharing your values. It also helps to explain your reasons for wanting your children to desist. If you forbid street language and tell them, 'I never want to hear you saying things like that again', they may take you at your word. Your daughter or son will try to be more discreet when you or other adults are around. Young people love to follow directions exactly when it suits their purpose. Most adolescents make an effort not to let adults hear street language.

Some do so secure in the knowledge that they are re-
belling safely. By following instructions not to let a parent
hear crude language they give themselves the freedom to
be as vulgar as they like with their peers. If they are
caught out they can fall back on the argument that they
were doing exactly what they were told.

Respecting privacy

Let me make it very clear that I am not advocating
snooping or eavesdropping on private conversations. I am
writing about ordinary situations where youngsters speak
loudly and forget there are adults present who can
overhear. In these situations young people may even have
a hidden agenda. They may unconsciously be attempting
to provoke some kind of reaction from a parent. They
want to know your views on sex, contraception, abortion
and romance. Do not disappoint them. Tell them honestly
what you think and how you feel. They need to understand why you hold these values. Tell them why you think
as you do. Your openness will help them recognise how
they feel too. It also helps them learn how to express
safely what they themselves are feeling.

I cannot stress enough how vitally important it is for
a parent to be respectful of a daughter's or son's privacy.
The only exception to this is if a parent suspects a young
person is using drugs. Then in the interests of safety it
may be necessary to search for illegal substances. If
parents had any idea of the trauma some children go
through in an effort to keep personal things private they
would act in a more respectful way. For example, one of
the very common worries young girls have about getting

their first period is, 'Who will Mum tell?' A surprising number of girls are worried that: 'My mum will tell everyone.'

TREATING GIRLS AND BOYS DIFFERENTLY

It is interesting that families deal with girls and boys very differently in adolescence. Surely a boy's first wet dream is as significant an event in his life as a girl's first period is for her. It is the visible sign that he is becoming a man. Yet it is kept very private. Hardly any boys tell a parent when they have their first nocturnal emission. Girls usually tell when they have their first period. Of course this is necessary because of the need for sanitary protection. It goes without saying that parents should treat these important events in the life of a girl or boy with great sensitivity.

Many adults do not show sufficient respect for the way young people think or feel. The jargon, the crude and vulgar language adolescents use to describe the body and bodily functions, may indicate a failure to respect their own bodies. It is sad that so many parents and teachers use this language barrier as an excuse for not talking to young people about sex. Time and time again adults tell me, 'We need to be educated. We don't know what the kids are talking about. We don't understand the peer pressure they are under.' They do not, but that should not stop them from opening up a discussion.

Many parents who give children otherwise good information about the facts of life do not know what to say about crude language or early sexual behaviour like intimate kissing. The answer is that they should spell out the harm that crude and vulgar attitudes to sex can do. Such comments as: 'I feel worried when I see you acting so grown-up with the opposite sex; you may not be aware of what you are getting yourself into; I don't want to hear you using those crude terms to describe genitals; ugly jargon makes the body seem ugly' may even give the child the confidence to resist deleterious peer pressure. Explain the language and terminology you would prefer them to use: 'The word is "breasts", not "tits" and the like.'

SEXUAL ATTRACTION

Few parents encourage young people to become familiar with their own sexual responsiveness. It should be explained that sexual attraction has a lot more to do with hormones than it has to do with real love. They should be informed that they are physically ready for sex long before they have the emotional maturity to deal with powerful sexual feelings, that sexual attraction is good and to be enjoyed as part of God's plan to draw women and men together in different kinds of friendship. It is helpful when parents acknowledge how intense adolescents' feelings are. Be willing to discuss all the repercussions of unmarried sexual activity. Adolescents need to learn that casual sex does not just affect people physically, that it has emotional and spiritual consequences as well.

It is essential to educate young people that they give messages not just verbally but also with facial expressions and body language. Boys who get their sex education from the media are more likely to misread a girl's body language. Quite naturally curious about women and sex, lots of young lads look for information from videos and in sex magazines. (These are more readily available than parents think. The top shelves in most newsagents have a wide selection of salacious reading material, nearly all directed at males.) A staple of these pornographic and erotic magazines is the insatiable woman who loves to be dominated.

Girls and boys are going to behave sexually as they grow into adulthood. The younger adolescents are when they begin to date, the greater the likelihood of frightening or bad experiences which may have serious long-term effects. Learning to deal with sexual pressures is a vital part of growing to maturity. Young people who feel pressured into behaving in sexually intimate ways need support and accurate information. Obviously it would help if they could talk to a compassionate, caring adult who would show an understanding of the problems. Sadly a very large number of young people feel there is no adult in whom they can confide. Believing that 'Nobody can understand; nobody has ever been through what I am going through' is a normal part of adolescence.

GREATER FREEDOM FOR GIRLS?

Sexual equality has encouraged women to take charge of their own lives and fertility. If a girl is attracted to a lad she now has the freedom to approach him or get her friends to ask him for a date. Some boys welcome this; others find it difficult to let women have the power that formerly belonged to males. Even twenty years ago strong moral standards governed behaviour. They protected teenagers from being subjected to the kinds of sexual harassment that are so common today. Hardly any modern young girl would think of protecting her virtue by professing a strong belief in virginity. Figures show that the greatest increase in pre-marital sex is among women. The old macho male standard that put pressure on lads to make female conquests is now characteristic of the behaviour of some younger women. Proving one's masculinity by acting like a stud must be exposed as gross exploitation.

As I have asserted several times, using another person sexually is never an acceptable option. No matter what social freedoms they think they possess, both girls and boys need to be taught refusal skills so that they are confident that they can be sexually assertive. All adolescents need to know how to cope when passion is aroused, and they cannot learn to deal with their intimacy needs in a healthy way without adult guidance. Some parents may find it extremely difficult or even impossible to educate their charges to meet these needs in non-genital ways and this is why parents must insist that these important issues be included in the curriculum for relationships and sexuality education programmes taught in schools.

Double Standard

Many adults are not sure whether they should teach their young people about contraception or not. They have accepted the popularly held belief that one cannot stop teenagers having sex and therefore believe their main duty is to teach them how to avoid being a party to an unwanted pregnancy and contracting STDs. Few parents are aware that this attitude on their part puts further pressure on their children to engage in sexual activity. Adolescents who are told, 'Don't you come back to me pregnant' pick up the underlying message: 'My parents think I am going to have sex; they expect me to do it.'

There is widespread confusion among adolescents regarding 'safe sex' and how to be sexually responsible. Influenced by AIDS prevention advertisements, many believe that to be responsible sexually means no more that avoiding unwanted pregnancy and sexually trans-mitted diseases. Some parents share this view while others are totally opposed to condom use. To add to this confusion, many adults give double messages: 'You shouldn't (have sex) but if you do, be sure to use pro-tection.' The dual standards of sexual behaviour that are so widely accepted in modern society bewilder ado-lescents. They are very aware of a number of sexual scandals that involved people whose public stance was for morality but who condoned different standards in private.

First love

Puberty is quickly followed by first love, which always involves strong new feelings. When girls and boys are able to share how they are feeling, they are better able to put their sexual desires into perspective. This encourages them to delay sexual activity. Young people need to understand that their overwhelmingly strong new sexual feelings are normal. Ideally this should happen through talking to parents. In reality a parent is often the last person a girl or boy will talk to about their burgeoning sexuality.

This is hardly surprising, because the majority of adolescents will project their own discomfort about discussing anything to do with sex on to Mum or Dad. We can teach young people to be more comfortable about sexuality by giving them a new understanding of both affective and genital sexuality. They will learn that when a woman relates as a woman she is relating as a sexual person. Her sexuality, that is her femininity, influences how she behaves. The same is true for men. When a man relates in a masculine way he is also relating sexually.

Parents of boys tend to be more aware of the radical changes in the attitudes of girls that have occurred in the past decade. Girls chase their sons. They telephone and call to the house without any shyness or inhibitions. In many instances the female attentions are premature and not that welcome. One result of this new sense of sexual equality is that parents must ensure that boys as well as girls are taught refusal skills.

Unless young people are taught to be assertive they will be vulnerable to unwelcome sexual pressure. I always tell young people to speak out immediately if someone touches them in any way that makes them feel uneasy or uncomfortable. If a lad puts his hand on a girl's knee, what usually happens? She remains silent but pushes the hand away. Half a minute later it is back. Again she pushes the hand away and again it comes back.

If she could have spoken out and said the obvious thing: 'Have you noticed you put your hand on my knee?' or 'Why did you put your hand on my knee?' the matter would then have been brought out into the open. She would have asserted her right not to be touched without

70

permission. By making it clear that she will not permit anyone to take advantage of her in little ways, she gains confidence in her ability to speak out about what she likes and dislikes. This is an essential skill and is the cornerstone for the communication that is required in respectful loving relationships. The same applies, in this age of increasing sexual equality, to boys in corresponding circumstances. When a parent recalls her own adolescence she is probably remembering back to a time when the awareness of sexual drives happened gradually. A young person could enjoy the thrill of being looked at with interest by the opposite sex long before dating was a possibility. Today, sexual awareness is thrust on young people by the media long before it has a meaning in their inner lives. As a result even young children may appear to be knowledgeable about sex, but this is deceptive. Even when they are clear on the basic facts, they still need opportunities to discuss their sexual feelings, to ask further questions. The question remains: have they the communication skills to do this?

5

PARENTS AND TEENAGERS

FAMILY VALUES

It is unfortunate that some teenage girls and boys feel guilty about their interest in sex. Sadly the attitude that sex is somehow dirty or shameful is still alive, despite the greater sexual freedom enjoyed in our society. Parents' values have been absorbed by adolescents without any conscious awareness on their part. Consequently the choices young people make about their sexual behaviour are not as original or free as they would like to believe. They are influenced by personal, family and religious values and by their own plans for education and a possible career.

Whether parents are married, single, separated or divorced, they have an enormous influence on young people. Parents' relationships have a great bearing on whether a teenager will consider marriage later on. Studies show that the sexual activity of adolescents is lowest in two-parent families, highest in lone-parent families, and in-between in remarried or blended families. In this matter parents have a greater influence on teenagers than their peers. Research has also shown that in a significant number of cases the earlier the mother's own first sexual experience and first birth take place, the earlier the daughter's first sexual experience is likely to occur.

Teenagers think that they are making free choices about their sexual behaviour. They are seldom aware of how they have been conditioned to live up to the expectations of their parents, their teachers, their religion, their peers and their society. The way young people feel about their family values, authority and the role models they admire, will affect their decisions regarding what is right to do or not do sexually.

LACK OF BASIC INFORMATION

It never ceases to surprise me how knowledgeable adolescents are about some things and yet how ignorant many of them are about how the human body works. Girls who have been dating for years still worry about trivial things: 'My friends all have their period for five days, and mine lasts only three. Is this normal?' or 'I am quite worried that one breast is a different size from the other.' Some boys worry about masturbation and there are those who still believe the old myth that it will make you blind. Girls are less concerned.

For many parents, teenage sexual fantasy was about the move from holding hands to a French kiss. Nowadays many adolescents have dispensed with these preliminaries altogether. Some therapists are concerned that petting is dying out and that the leap from a goodnight kiss to intercourse is too quick. If we accept that teenagers are sexually active then we do them a disservice if we fail to educate them about the importance of communication and foreplay for a woman.

MOOD SWINGS

Hormones are to blame for a lot of the turmoil of adolescence. Practically anything, it seems, can spark off a mood swing. Your apparently happy daughter can suddenly lash out angrily for no reason you can understand. Your son is full of confidence one minute, and the next he has become painfully self-conscious, pessimistic and morose. The growing-up period is not easy for either parents or children. One week your adolescent is acting all grown-up, full of confidence, demanding independence and freedom and resenting all parental restraint. The following week (or the same afternoon) he is acting like a spoilt, helpless child, needing comfort, reassurance and support. Again, blame their hormones.

Of course teenagers do grow out of this stage and begin to see themselves more rationally. There is, however, no fixed time for this to happen. The way they describe themselves will give you a clue as to what is going on. In the early stages of puberty they will describe themselves in terms of appearance. As they mature they will describe themselves less defensively – probably in terms of personality. They have an awful lot with which to contend. Dealing with peer pressure and moods, feeling mixed up and unsure of oneself, and worrying about being attractive to the opposite sex, cannot be easy. There is often a fair amount of confusion about sexuality too. Both girls and boys worry about what is normal in the teenage years. Few young people feel comfortable talking to parents about their sexuality. Although many parents are willing to talk, teenagers tell me they feel safer to confide in a stranger rather than someone they know. It gives them the freedom to reveal behaviour and attitudes they could not admit to a parent.

MATURITY

There is no one age for adolescents to reach maturity. Girls usually mature earlier than boys. Around the time of a girl's first period she begins to experience changes in her self-image. She feels different and unsettled. These feelings of restlessness and being at odds with oneself are likely to last for three or four years. Adolescents are extremely sensitive to what others think, and in the early stages of puberty both girls and boys suffer from very low self-esteem. This is hardly surprising when you take into account all that is happening to them. There is little doubt but that the greasy hair, spots, new body shape and hormonal upheaval make life difficult. As well there is no precise age for a girl to get her first period or a boy his first wet dream. The fact that one young person begins early and another late has nothing to do with intelligence. It helps to explain why some fourteen or fifteen-year-olds are still so sensitive.

In the early stages of adolescence young people are very self-disparaging about how they look and dress. Parents and teachers are probably all too familiar with the obsession they seem to have with their appearance. Mirrors and other reflective surfaces become terribly important. A spot check takes on a brand new meaning.

A tiny pimple that an adult would have difficulty in seeing may seem like a huge blemish to a teenager. Never underestimate the sensitivity of a youngster who genuinely feels a spot is an absolute disaster. A tiny pustule can seem enormous to highly sensitive teenagers. If they feel it spoils their appearance it can make them feel unattractive and undesirable – social rejects.

BELONGING
A very common problem with girls in their early teenage years is the feeling of being left out of, or rejected by their peer group. Girls who reach puberty early tend to be drawn to each other and form a group. They have 'grown-up' interests in common. Some move on from childhood friendships that may have lasted since kindergarten. The friends they leave behind are often devastated. They do not understand why their best friend no longer wants to play. Other girls become so tied up with boys when they begin to date that their female friends feel ignored. Once the romance ends they expect to take up with their old friends again. Some are welcomed back into the fold; others are excluded and go through a painful time trying to find a group which will accept them.

The fear of being rejected and thrown out of a group is very real for girls. Those who sympathise with a girl trying to get back in are often afraid to speak out in her favour. The risk of being excluded if the gang leader refuses to allow the girl to rejoin is too great. Boys do not tend to have similar problems. The kind of communication skills that would help children develop the confidence to speak out courageously in these circumstances

should be part of every relationships education programme.

There is no denying that young people need relationships education that will help them to understand how
they have been conditioned to accept as normal behaviour
that is hurtful and damaging to others. Effective education programmes should contain elements that will
enable young people to explore their expectations of
relationships with friends and family. I think all students
should have the opportunity to discuss their ideas and
expectations of friendships with both their own and the
opposite sex in group situations. They must be made
aware that they all have intimacy needs and shown how
to meet these needs in appropriate non-genital ways. It
is widely accepted that a great deal of teenager promiscuity is due to the fact that many young people have
never learned how to meet their affectionate needs in non-
sexual ways.

CLOTHES

Every parent knows that clothes are important to adolescents. 'Looking good' usually means different things to
parents and children. They seldom agree on what being
well-dressed means. I think it is possible to get agreement
on compromises about clothes but I would never underestimate how terrible it is for a teenager to wear something wrong, something that does not fit the current
image that is acceptable to the peers.

Young people have confided to me that they feel
freakish when they get it wrong. It can be incredibly
damaging to their self-esteem when people they regard

as friends mock them. Having your friends tell you to your face that what you are wearing is acceptable and then to find they are laughing at you behind your back is a bigger problem for girls than for boys. Young people need to be able to discuss this aspect of peer pressure in classroom or group situations. Teachers can open up a discussion in a non-threatening way: 'Does wearing branded jeans make you OK? Are you OK if you have a fashionable hairstyle?' Could you have these and not be a good person?'

A TIME OF TRANSITION FOR PARENTS

Often when teenagers are going through the transition from childhood to adulthood, parents are in the throes of the mid-life crisis. This is a period when adults tend to have their own special needs and problems. It is a time when both parents and teenagers have different concerns with hormonal upheaval and changing body shapes. Mum may be heading towards the menopause and although there is nothing hormonal about the so-called male menopause many men become cranky at this time – some studies suggest two thirds or more. Dad may be contend-ing with a loss of fitness and an expanding waistline. Fathers who arrange rather than comb their hair can be a source of huge embarrassment to some adolescents.

Teenagers are fine-tuned to a parent's ambivalence about body-image and sexuality. If a boy has never heard his father comment agreeably on his mother's appearance he may find it difficult to tell a girlfriend how attractive he finds her. In order to affirm a woman, a man needs to know what he thinks and how he feels. Many men were brought up to deny, ignore and repress their feelings. They are not to blame for this, but being complimentary to a spouse or partner does not come naturally to them. If Dad does not know that talking creates a sense of intimacy for Mum, how can his son be sensitive to the need of a woman to feel good emotionally before making love?

FALLING IN AND OUT OF LOVE

Falling in love for young people has far more to do with their hormones than it has to do with real love. Boys are more likely to be sexually motivated by hormones than girls, who are much more influenced by social controls. Parents should explain that falling in love is wonderful and that the intense feelings of attraction are to be enjoyed, but that most teenage romances do not last. Love for teenagers is motivated mainly by sexual attraction and it is advisable to encourage teenagers to do their socialising within the relative safety of mixed groups. I say relative safety because this does not necessarily preclude a good deal of affectionate sexual interaction. There is, however, always the possibility of deeper romantic emotional attachments occurring for older teenagers, especially ones who have reached sexual maturity. Early adolescent attachments are short-lived. One piece of research put the length of the average sixteen-year-old's romance at forty-five days.

Being head over heels in love involves feelings of ecstatic euphoria or ecstatic desperation for teenagers, feelings which are seldom experienced in so intense a way again. Broken romances can seem devastating; for some teenagers it is as if the world has ended and there is no light in the darkness. Few parents are prepared for the stunned and tearful grief that follows. Some recoveries are almost miraculous – a fresh romance wipes away the tears – while other young people take a longer time to recover. Parents of bereft teenagers need to be patient and allow them the space to get over the hurt in their own time. They should allow as long as is necessary to mend a broken heart.

GOOD SEX?

There is a lot of truth in the old saying that men give love in order to get sex while women give sex in order to get love. If a woman does not feel emotionally close to her spouse or partner, she may respond physically but it is certain that she will not feel fulfilled sexually. This is true regardless of the experience or sexual techniques used by her lover. Teenagers need to learn that good sex requires loving commitment, that sex is one of the means of deep communication between the sexes. Their success as lovers will depend on how well they communicate. Sex reflects the state of a couple's relationship; it is only as good as the relationship is at the time. If a woman is feeling angry with her spouse or partner it is very hard for her to make love. Males need to understand that for a great majority of women to have the fullest pleasure, the relationship needs to be right before lovemaking.

Studies show that a man's primary motive for choosing a woman is her physical attractiveness. It is hardly surprising then that a woman's body-image is an important part of her self-image. As a woman's body-image changes at the menopause or at puberty, so does her self-image. Some mothers who struggle to keep from putting on weight have mixed feelings when they see a teenage daughter's puppy fat drop away to reveal a firm, nubile figure. Admiration is sometimes tinged with envy and a hidden grieving for what might have been.

The mid-life period is a time when many couples reassess their priorities. Some review their couple relationship and find it wanting. The painful realisation dawns that it may be too late for certain dreams and ambitions to be realised. For many couples a good sex life is central to a happy, comfortable relationship. Infrequent sex is associated with problems. The wife may may be turned off sex when the husband focuses on the physical side to the exclusion of the emotional side. We have seen that a lot of fathers do not have the freedom to share their personal thoughts and feelings. Is it any wonder that teenage boys assume that this is how men are supposed to be?

Many men believe that to be masculine they must control their feelings. Studies show that a father cannot make a son masculine in this way. Putting pressure on boys to be masculine often has the opposite effect. In families where the father is masculine and also loving and supportive and able to share in caring for the children, both girls and boys learn to be sexually confident.

BORING?

Most adolescents judge their parents' relationship to be b-o-r-i-n-g. Many are convinced that their parents no longer have sex. One can understand why they think like this. Teenagers spend a lot of time thinking about sex and live in anticipation of enjoying exciting, passionate, earth-shattering sex. In fantasy, innocent situations are made into erotic encounters. The suggestion that parents might share sexual pleasure is dismissed. It would come as quite an eye-opener for teenagers to discover that in general married people enjoy better sex than unmarried couples or those having affairs. In 1992 the *American National Survey of Families and Households* polled 13,000 adults. They found that long-term monogamous couples made love twice as often as singles in the same age group. They also reported overall higher satisfaction with their sex lives. Similar results were found in other surveys.

It is astonishing that so many young people believe their parents are too old to have sex. Pre-teens are often quite uncomfortable at the thought of their parents enjoying intercourse. Teenagers who should know better suggest that sometime between twenty-eight and thirty-five years their parents give up having sex. By then they assume they are too old and too tired to manage to raise any passion. Most of them know that boys reach their sexual peak around the age of eighteen. Not as many are aware that many women reach their sexual peak much later, around the age of thirty-five.

The idea that sex holds no pleasure for couples once their childbearing years are coming to an end is another old myth that needs to be contradicted. One of the best-kept secrets of our time is that sexual arousal and enjoyment can be positively affected by the menopause. The freedom to enjoy sex without fear of pregnancy gives older women a new lease of life. Many men are under the illusion that women do not enjoy sex as much as they do. They need to learn that human females are the sexiest female creatures alive. When conditions for lovemaking are right they can enjoy sex every bit as much as, if not more than men. Their orgasms last longer too.

DIFFERENT SEXES; DIFFERENT NEEDS

Young people need to be educated about the difference between the sexual responsiveness of women and men. Sex makes men feel good under almost any circumstances. This is not the case for women. Surveys in women's magazines show that many women would prefer to be cuddled and have a sensual experience than have full intercourse. They need to feel they are loved before they are ready for intimacy. Ideally a girl wants a partner to have a commitment to her before she becomes intimately involved. Teenagers need to understand that the sexes have different emotional needs as well. Boys must be educated to realise that a woman wants to feel loved before she is ready for sex. She needs the reassurance of knowing that a man is not just using her for her body. She needs him to show her that he cares. How does a man do this? By talking, sharing personal thoughts and feelings, and generally creating a feeling of intimacy.

It is really important for girls to know that they deserve better than a selfish partner who is only out to satisfy himself. A partner who genuinely cares will be anxious to please. It is true that boys get sexually aroused quicker than girls. It is equally true that men who make good lovers know how to take things slowly and sensuously. They are sensitive to a partner and able to pick up both verbal and non-verbal cues. Teenagers need to be made aware that lovemaking involves communication at a very deep level that goes beyond words.

Honest communication is the secret ingredient in good relationships. Sadly many, many men do not know how to talk to their wives or partners in an intimate way. When I work in co-educational schools I do an exercise with teenagers. I ask the boys, 'What do you think women are looking for from men?' They usually suggest things like, 'Looks, a huge six-pack [abdominal muscles are known as a six-pack], bulging biceps and a big dick.' Some will add: 'Girls want love.' The girls are outraged and they complain that boys are immature. 'Everything they say is sexually orientated.' Some add 'perverted'. 'They only want to get their little bit so they can boast about how good they are.'

Then I get the girls to tell the boys how they want to be treated. Almost all the girls favour a fellow who is not immature or pushy about sex. They say they want to be with a boy who has a good personality. Many want lads with a spirit of adventure and daring in them. They want to be treated 'nice around his friends'. They want a boy who takes time to talk. Some would like a boy to give them presents. Other feel presents would make them uncomfortable. Many girls would love to have a romantic relationship but feel this would make the boys uneasy.

Asked what girls want from boys, a lad in one school handed me this note. 'First of all most girls want the big dick, twenty inches of hairy hardness, pressurised ejaculation system pumping out two tons of crude sperm.' I said, 'I feel very uncomfortable with this kind of language. I find it crude and offensive, but I am going to assume that it is motivated by a need for accurate information. The size of a penis has little bearing on whether a man is able to give his wife pleasure. Good sex has far more to do with a loving relationship and good communication than with the size of a man's genitals.' Behind the bravado of that answer was a very insecure boy who needed to be reassured.

WRONG ATTITUDES

Boys and men have a lot of insecurity about penis size. It would be easy to blame the boy for his lack of respect, but before judging him it might be wise to ask where he got his sex education. Is he to blame for using the language with which he is familiar to talk about sexuality? Respectful attitudes to people or sex or property have to be learned.

I am not surprised when immature boys make rude sexual comments but I am deeply concerned when not enough effort is made to challenge wrong attitudes. I believe there are thousands of teenagers with crude, vulgar, disrespectful attitudes to sex that need to be contradicted. Parents need to be aware that some boys harass girls by making personal comments and thereby make their lives a misery. Teachers need to recognise this as a form of bullying, and students must be encouraged to speak out when it happens. If verbal harassment is not nipped in the bud it can become physical.

PARENTS NOT PREPARED FOR ADOLESCENCE

The teenage years can be time of anxiety in a family, especially when concern about children's safety leads to controlling or rejecting behaviour. Research shows that parents are generally not well prepared for the adolescence of the first child, and fathers who feel uncomfortable at the emerging sexuality of their daughters may become very authoritarian or distant. This can happen without any conscious awareness of what they are doing to either themselves or their daughters.

It is foolish for parents to assume that by looking back on their own teenage years they can understand what it is like to be an adolescent today. A teenager's life today bears no resemblance to that of an adolescent twenty or more years ago. Since that time there have been fundamental changes in society's attitudes to sexuality. These changes make it exceptionally difficult for parents to know what to do for the best.

Most adults cannot determine what is considered acceptable behaviour among teenagers. Many agree when they are told that their attitudes are old-fashioned. Some parents find it helpful to compare ideas with other parents. This may work in some cases but in others it may make parental decisions even harder. If the parents consulted are more liberal or more conservative than the advice seekers, the latter can end up more confused than ever.

Teenagers who want to grow into independent adults need to examine the values of parents, society and the Church in order to determine their own values. During this questioning process, many rebel temporarily and seem to reject parental values, especially with regard to sex and money. Conflict and controversy are a necessary part of adolescence, and though almost every parent worries about arguments when there are teenagers in the house, it is necessary for them to understand that this is a normal part of the maturing process. Not alone is some conflict normal with teenagers but it is both healthy and necessary.

REASSURANCE AND ENCOURAGEMENT

Teenagers are in constant need of reassurance. They worry about being attractive to the other sex. Parents can help them to feel good about themselves by mentioning the favourable things they see. They should recognise when their children make an effort, and comment favourably: 'I appreciate your phoning to explain why you were delayed.' 'It was great to see you were tactful when you refused to go out with John.' 'I'm not disappointed with your results. I know you tried. Your best effort is always good enough.'

Sometimes parents assume that young people feel good when they are complimented, unaware that the words that were meant to reassure may put them under pressure. 'You were good to ring. I always feel anxious when you are delayed' may be intended to affirm, but it may not achieve that intention. A super-sensitive teenager may hear only 'You made me anxious'; an adolescent fine-tuned to criticism might overlook 'You were good' and react to 'You were late.' So much teenage conflict happens because parents and teenagers pick up messages that were never intended.

Young people can feel put down when a parent sets out to build them up. 'You did really well. I am proud of you' may be interpreted as, 'They are only proud of me when I achieve.' There is a subtle difference between reassurances and compliments. Many adolescents go through a period where they almost seem to dismiss supportive comments. If parents make the effort to change those compliments into reassuring statements they could get a very different reception.

Unhappily there are endless possibilities for misunderstanding among people who love each other. With the best will in the world it is difficult to communicate honestly and openly with another person. Words are never heard in isolation. How the meaning of the words heard is understood is also influenced by self-worth and by what is seen and assumed by the hearer. The sad thing about miscommunication is that it so often happens between people who genuinely care for each other and have no desire to hurt or deceive.

6

FAMILY COMMUNICATION

SEX DIFFERENCES IN COMMUNICATION

Good communication is essential in any relationship. It is the lifeblood that nurtures love. Studies by linguists, sociologists and psychologists over the last twenty years show that differences in the ability of the sexes to communicate are responsible for many of the problems that are common in couple relationships. The differences in how women and men communicate are so pronounced that at times it can seem as if they are speaking different languages. This is not due to conditioning alone. There are basic physiological differences between women's and men's brains.

In the neocortex, the area of the brain essential for conscious thought, a bundle of nerve fibres called the *corpus callosum* connects the two hemispheres of the brain. The left hemisphere has the logical properties. The powers of imagery and intuition reside in the right hemisphere. The *corpus callosum* sends messages between the two hemispheres. It appears to be thicker in the female, indicating that women's brains have a greater number of connecting channels than their male counterparts.

The left side of a girl's brain develops more rapidly than that of a boy's brain. This is why girls in general learn to talk earlier, have a better vocabulary and more accurate pronunciation, and read earlier. The right side of the brain develops faster in boys. They enjoy earlier visual, spatial, logical and perceptual development. Some studies show that women have more developed left brains, men more developed right brains. There is no agreement on whether this is as a result of nature or nurture. Some scientists argue that women and men think and act differently from one another because of biological differences. Others believe they do so because of the way they have been reared. The jury is still out on the nature versus nurture debate.

In one study that examined the speech of teenagers it was found that male teenage speech was more forceful, dominating, boastful, blunt, authoritarian and to the point than female speech. Girls' speech was found to be gentler, friendlier, faster, more emotional and more enthusiastic than boys'. Linguist Dr Deborah Tannen suggests that the way to bridge the communication gap between the sexes is to acknowledge that women and men speak different languages and to start to accept those differences.

WOMEN'S PROBLEM-SOLVING

There is a wealth of evidence to show that a great deal of stress and misunderstanding between couples who love each other is caused by communication difficulties. It is the most natural thing in the world for a girl or woman who has a problem to want to talk to her boyfriend or partner about her difficulty. Sadly, few people have been taught that listening is a vitally important component of good communication. If a man listens to a woman with acceptance, she feels heard and this creates a sense of intimacy for her. Men need to understand how important the talking process is for helping a woman feel closeness with a partner.

Communication skills can be taught and learned. Most men assume that when a woman shares a problem she is looking for advice. This is seldom so. Usually she is seeking to process information in the way that is natural for a woman. By discussing what she is thinking and how she is feeling, a woman successfully identifies the exact nature of the situation in which she finds herself. As she talks about the problem she begins to work out what her options are. The most helpful thing for a woman with a problem is to feel listened-to and have what she says reflected back to her in the words of the other person. The technical name for this skill is active listening, and it mirrors back to the woman the choices she is considering. As she talks she will frequently look at the pros and cons of the options open to her. She explores her choices as she talks about them. Just by talking things out she achieves a sense of intimacy and the clarity to reach a decision. Both sexes need to understand how differences in their patterns of communication affect couple relationships.

MEN'S PROBLEM-SOLVING

When a man has a problem to solve he feels very differently from a woman. If he needs expert advice he will discuss the problem with an authority on the matter. Otherwise he prefers to go away and think about what options are open to him. The last thing in the world that he wants before he has come to a decision on his own is to talk about what is bothering him. He will not feel ready to talk about his difficulty until he has decided on a solution.

It would make a huge difference if women understood that when a man has a problem he needs time to think about it before he is ready to talk about the difficulty. Girls need to understand that if they have a problem with a boyfriend it is essential to discuss the problem, but after *and only after* he has had time to go away and think about the solution. Boys need to comprehend that when a woman is worried she needs to talk about what worries her. When both sexes understand that they communicate differently they can learn to appreciate these differences in a positive way. A woman who understands her need to talk might suggest to a partner, 'I am worried about this and would like to discuss it. You probably need time to think it out, so let's chat about it at the weekend. How about after dinner on Saturday?' Talking things out is more usually initiated by a female partner. Men seldom invite such discussions. When a man is asked to participate it is perfectly OK for him to ask to defer the discussion. Boys need to be taught that it is acceptable to say something like, 'I want to think about that for a bit. Could you leave it with me and we can talk about it tomorrow evening', or whenever is a suitable time.

MORE THAN WORDS

Only about 7 per cent of communication has to do with words. The other 93 per cent has to do with facial expression, body language and tone of voice. Good communication involves assumptions and perceptions as well as words. What we hear another person say is coloured by expectations that come from our prior experiences in similar situations. We make assumptions based on whether we think the speaker cares for us or not. Problems arise when people do not realise this and treat assumptions as if they were facts.

Say for example a young couple were dating and when they met he forgot to wish her a happy birthday. She might assume: 'If he truly cared for me he would remember my birthday.' If she thinks like this she is bound to feel upset. She reads his omission as a lack of caring. On the other hand she might choose to think: 'He hasn't really forgotten. I bet he is planning some wonderful surprise later.' Instead of feeling that her special day has been overlooked, she allows this expectation to build up in her a sense of excited anticipation. It is important to understand that the words said are only a tiny part of communication. What is not said also communicates something. Those unspoken expectations also have a profound effect on how people relate.

The assumptions we make about the intentions behind the words that are said impact on our feelings too. If a teenage girl hears her boyfriend tell her he loves her she has choices regarding what she understands him to convey. She might think, 'He says that to every girl; he is saying it only because he wants to be intimate', or she may believe, 'He really means it. He truly loves me.'

If she believes that he tells everyone he dates he loves her, his protestations of love will have little value. If she assumes that he is saying it to soften her up for later intimacy, she might feel amused if she has the confidence to refuse his advances; or she might feel angry and disrespected at the idea that he plans to use her body for his own pleasure. If she feels he is expressing a genuine, deeply felt emotion she will probably feel thrilled and excited. Her feelings come from the way she thinks about his intentions.

The way we hear the words that are said or interpret the actions of others is also influenced by our own life experiences. Say for example a boy came from a family where he saw his father give his mother flowers regularly. Giving flowers to a woman would be a natural thing for him to do. However, if he presented flowers to a girl who never saw her mother get a bunch of flowers in her life, she might read things into the gift that he did not intend. She might assume that the gift of flowers had special significance and indicated a deep romantic interest on his part. He is unlikely to be aware of the assumptions she has made or the expectations of the relationship that were kindled by the flowers.

There is, then, considerable potential for conflict when couples have different expectations of each other. Most couples do not enjoy the kind of honest communication which allows them to speak openly about their hopes and dreams. When two people are unaware that they have different expectations of each other, problems can easily arise. Disappointment is almost guaranteed if one party expects the other to be a mind-reader. It is astonishing to find highly intelligent people who have a sense of grievance against a partner who should have known something despite never having been told.

MISUNDERSTANDINGS, EXPECTATIONS AND ASSUMPTIONS

Failure to communicate honestly is the root cause of dissatisfaction in troubled relationships. A lot of unnecessary pain is caused because people attribute thoughts and feelings to others based on their own expectations. They wrongly assume that others understand the world in exactly the same way as they do. There is a story told about a teenage boy who was in trouble with his mother for going out when he was grounded. 'You knew I was going out and you said nothing to stop me,' he accused his mother angrily. She denied any knowledge of lifting the ban. 'You saw me ironing my blue shirt,' he said, 'and you know that when I iron a shirt on Saturday night I always go out.'

Similarly, a girl who has taken a lot of trouble to dress up for her boyfriend might invite him to compliment her, either by asking, 'What do you think?' or by doing a model's twirl. Many lads feel very uncomfortable when put on the spot in this way. They are not sure what is expected of them. An embarrassed 'You look great' drawn from a reluctant lad may seem endearing to one young woman; it may disappoint another who expected some more extravagant compliment. Yet the facial expression and tone of voice used could totally transform those mundane words into meaning something very special.

Young people need to be educated to understand how

easily the words they use can convey meanings that were not intended. They need to be reminded that only part of the message is given with words and that sometimes body language can contradict the words said. Adolescents need to be taught how to communicate clearly and unambiguously. The old joke about the girl who says 'Don't. Stop! Don't. Stop! Don't stop, don't stop, don't stop', shows how easy it is to give mixed messages. It is important for young people to communicate clearly about their behavioural boundaries. They need to be aware of how important it is to be explicit about how far they want to go, so that the other person does not think they are protesting without meaning it. Saying something like, 'Don't do that' is not specific enough. It is better to explain clearly what is unacceptable. 'I do not want you to put your hand under my shirt. I am happy to kiss you but I do not want to go any further.'

GOOD LISTENING

Good listening is a vitally important part of relationships and sexuality education. Parents and teachers need to help girls and boys to put the sexual information they have within a moral and spiritual framework. They cannot do this without guidance from a trusted adult with good listening skills. Non-judgemental reflective listening is a very necessary but undervalued part of sex education. Theoretically it is easier for a listener who is compassionate and understanding to be trusted by a young person. In reality young people are unlikely to be as honest with someone who is personally known to them as they would be with a stranger.

One of the most difficult areas for adults who are working with teenagers is how to communicate their values in a convincing way. It is not enough for a listener to pay careful attention to the words alone. The feelings involved need to be picked up too. Reading about this makes it sound very artificial. It seems unnatural at first when learning this skill. With practice it becomes easier. Young people learn good communication skills remarkably quickly and become proficient in their use.

A majority of teenagers believe it is perfectly all right to have safe sex if you love someone and act responsibly. Many parents will find this impossible to accept. For many adults sexual responsibility has only one meaning – avoiding pre-marital sex. For most teenagers it means using contraceptive protection to avoid an unwanted pregnancy or STDs. The life-threatening consequences of having sex with different partners are too serious to ignore. The best way to counter such ideas is to challenge young people to think about their own values. This makes for a valuable learning experience. Parents and teachers are failing in their duty if they cannot prevail upon adolescents to examine the serious long-term consequences of promiscuous behaviour.

A good way to open the topic is to say how you feel or simply to look for information: 'I am worried about teenage promiscuity. Can I check with you? Is it true that the majority of teenagers believe it is OK for a person to have sex *every time* he or she is in love?' The *'every time'* discourages a simple yes – or no – answer. It invites further exploration of the topic and is unlikely to be taken as a personal question. Asked in a gentle, conversational tone of voice, the question has the potential for developing the conversation and exploring other important questions about sexual behaviour. It is important to invite young people to consider such questions as:

- How do teenagers decide the feeling is real love?
- Does society regard women and men who are sexually active in the same way or is their behaviour judged differently?
- Are girls who fall out of love likely to regret that they had sex? What about boys?
- Adolescent romances seldom last into adulthood. How many relationships do you think that the average young person would have before settling down: three, five, seven, ten or more?
- If young people have a number of serious relationships is it all right if they have sex with all the different partners?
- Would people who had a number of sexual partners find it easy to convince spouses that they could remain faithful in marriage?

Questions like these challenge teenagers to examine their attitudes to teenage relationships, unmarried pregnancy and serial monogamy. It brings them face to face with their own values, or lack of values, about love and sex and life. It encourages them to contradict the sexually permissive attitudes that are so widely accepted as the norm. Reflective questions get them to think about the way they value themselves. Through good listening on the part of significant adults young people can come to a sense of their own sacredness. It even helps them to understand in a different way religious teaching that is opposed to casual sex.

IMPOSING PARENTAL VALUES

This open-ended way of communicating about sexual behaviour may be unacceptable to a parent who strongly believes in virginity. Her first instinct might be to lay down the law and demand that sex be saved for marriage. One has to question how effective this approach is in making young people sexually responsible. If the young person has been influenced by advertisements for 'safe sex' and does not share his parent's values he is unlikely to respond to his parent's prohibition on genital intimacy. She can insist that her directive be obeyed but she cannot enforce her wishes. The reality is that those young people who decide to have sex will make sure that a parent is not around to stop them.

Some parents who have rigid attitudes try to control behaviour by using authority. Attempting to impose moral values on young people without involving them in the decision-making process is disrespectful and self-defeating. A far better way to encourage morally responsible behaviour is to allow young people to make informed choices based on their own values and convictions. It is essential that they are in possession of accurate information first.

Other less traditionally-minded parents may feel differently about virginity. Convinced that you cannot stop young people from having sex, they make an effort to protect teenagers with accurate information about contraception and the use of condoms. Neither of these approaches is ideal. Parents who regard themselves as broad-minded are unaware that teenagers are put under pressure to act sexually by too liberal expectations. Studies show that when a girl enjoys good communication with her mother she is likely to delay sexual activity and is more likely to use contraception. Boys who talk to their fathers about sexual topics are more likely to be sexually active.

TO WHOM CAN TEENAGERS TALK?

There is no doubt that girls and boys need to discuss their burgeoning sexuality during puberty, adolescence and even young adulthood. Every parent knows how important it is for teenagers to feel they belong in the peer group. Unfortunately peer-group support often encourages premature sexual behaviour that is contrary to parental wishes. Ideally most parents want young people to enjoy being friends with the other sex before they have an intimate relationship. They would like them to take time to get to know one another as friends and get the communication right with their partners before they think of becoming sexually involved.

Expert advice tells us that adults who share their opinions and discuss their values and beliefs influence young people to delay sexual activity. This is all very well for those who communicate well, but not all families do. Many independent-minded adolescents set out to have a very different kind of couple relationship from their parents'. Few experts suggest what to do when young people recognise that their parents do not communicate well. It is seldom acknowledged that some young people wisely reject parental recommendations.

Once a sexual dimension is introduced into a relationship, parental concerns about the physical, emotional and spiritual wellbeing of teenagers tend to be ignored. I am not convinced that girls and boys have any desire to talk either to their parents or to class teachers about such emotionally sensitive topics. They are far more likely to open up to a visiting teacher or counsellor than to a person they see every day. There is a great need for students to have the freedom to discuss sexual issues in an open and confidential environment with an understanding, non-judgemental adult. If they are not given this opportunity in school, many of them will be dependent on their peers for advice on their love lives.

Young people in a couple relationship do not develop the skills to communicate about their sexual needs and desires in a vacuum. They need to be taught. They need to be given a language through which to discuss sexuality. It is good for a student to discuss in a family situation the questions raised in the section in this chapter on good communication. The benefits are far greater in a class, where students discuss the questions with a facilitator who is trained to listen. The chances of challenging value-free attitudes to sexuality and contradicting hurtful attitudes to sex are far greater when teenagers work out the consequences of these behaviours for themselves.

CAN FEELINGS BE TRUSTED?

Young people assume that their parents would not be comfortable talking to them even when they are willing and eager to do so. Some girls and boys feel they cannot talk to their parents on any personal matter at all. Others may claim to have a good relationship with their parents but feel that when it comes to a discussion about sexual feelings and behaviour: 'I couldn't talk to either of my parents. They wouldn't understand. They would only tell me not to do it.' Adolescents need to be encouraged to question such feelings. How can they know whether this is true of their parents unless they risk finding out? It is helpful when a parent invites a child to talk. One way to do this is to be vulnerable and to share the concerns that you had when you were their age.

I suspect that many teenagers would be surprised at how open and positive their parents' attitudes to sexuality actually are. It is essential for teenagers to recognise that their wrong assumptions create obstacles to good family communication. For example, adolescents are seldom aware that the feelings and thinking they attribute to their parents may be their own projected feelings and expectations. Of course their ability to discuss these is powerfully influenced by the nature of the relationships in the home and by their own early learning experiences within the family.

Most young people are unaware that what they feel emotionally is deeply influenced by the learned expectations they have of relationships. When parents enjoy good communication skills they give children a sense of being heard. This results in the child feeling accepted. It makes it safe for him to express and explore his feelings. Learning to listen to and trust one's own feelings is an essential skill. A person who fails to acquire this skill cannot identify either his own feelings or the feelings of others. This inability to recognise feelings diminishes one's capability to listen well. If one person does not

understand the experience the other is sharing, it inter-
feres with communication.

In some families, parents ignore or dismiss the feelings
of children as if they were unimportant. In others,
children are encouraged to be open and communicative.
Children who have not been listened to adequately are
likely to grow into adolescents who are out of touch with
their feelings. As teenagers they are likely to have poor
communication skills and be more afraid and anxious, as
well as more aggressive and violent than those who can
talk about their problems. A child whose feelings are not
respected learns to handle difficult situations by repressing, denying or ignoring those feelings. This damages his
ability to relate. The ability to communicate is deeply
influenced by early learning experiences, observation,
awareness of feelings and respectful listening.

UNCLEAR MESSAGES
Young people do not always realise how simple it is to
receive or give an incorrect message. It is as easy to say
or hear the wrong thing as it is to misread body language
and jump to the wrong conclusion. When powerful sexual
feelings are involved the possibilities of malcommuni-
cation increase. This is particularly true when women and
men do not talk openly about their expectations. For
example, a boy hears his girlfriend say she loves him. She
intends to convey that she enjoys the closeness of being
held and cuddled. Influenced by his erupting hormones,
he may hear her admission of love as an invitation to
further intimacy. If he has the expectation that a couple
who love each other show it by having intercourse he may

make sexual advances. Teenage boys who believe that sexual desires are too powerful to control put pressure on girls to have sex. Adolescents need to be alerted as to how their behaviour is influenced by their own expectation of romantic situations. They need to understand that their body language, their posture and the clothes they wear communicate messages about them that are open to misinterpretation. Many young girls believe that one needs to dress sexily to be attractive to boys. Children as young as ten or eleven years of age who dress in sexy clothes do not have the maturity to deal with older children who leer at them.

Both sexes need to be educated in refusal skills. They need to learn how to give clear 'yes' and 'no' messages. A girl who feels uncomfortable when a boy is trying to touch her intimately might say, 'I'm not ready yet.' She may be unaware that he could hear the words as a promise. He might wait ten minutes and be devastated when he tries again and she gets upset. It is never too early to teach children effective communication skills. By the time they are dating they need to feel confident that they can be sexually assertive, both positively and negatively. They need to be taught how to give messages about their experience, feelings and needs. They need to be aware of how to receive such personal sharing about experience from another in a respectful way. Young people need to learn to differentiate between assertiveness, which is a respectful way of communicating, and aggression, which is not. When young people learn to communicate effectively they have learned the secret of nurturing successful, loving relationships.

7

THE SPIRITUALITY OF SEXUALITY

SPIRITUALITY

Tales of romance enjoy considerable popularity with women. The plots are standard: the couple meet; they share a certain chemistry that makes them fall madly, passionately in love. His eyes meet hers, and before they speak a single word we know their lives are irrevocably changed by that intense gaze. In fairy stories the happy couple get married and live happily ever after. In more modern romances they enjoy immediate gratification as they go to bed and instantly share earth-shattering sex.

The highly emotional and physical affairs described in popular fiction totally ignore the spiritual dimensions of sex. Yet it is widely accepted that to have a fully human life there has to be a spiritual as well as an emotional and physical dimension. There are as many different definitions of spiritual experiences as there are people. Most young people accept that being excited by a piece of art or admiring a sunset are spiritual experiences. Yet these same youngsters have the most enormous difficulty in understanding that there is a spiritual dimension to lovemaking. One reason for this is that the spirituality of sexuality has been largely ignored in Western society. Poor religious teaching is responsible for a lot of the negative attitudes to sex that are endemic in our culture.

It is quite astonishing that in a sexually permissive society there is still a lack of genuine freedom regarding sexual intimacy. Instead of being celebrated, sex is still equated with sin, sexual pleasure with decadence. If parents want to contradict negative attitudes and help young people to gain a positive attitude to sexual love they must first acknowledge the nature of their family beliefs. These powerfully influence the way in which young people think about relationships. It cannot be denied that there is confusion about sexual morality in many families that have double standards. Most people are unaware of how deeply their sexual attitudes have been influenced by the attitudes of their parents and grandparents. Studies show that dysfunctional patterns of behaviour can be traced back in families for five generations.

Spoken beliefs

Our family beliefs are incredibly strong. They teach us how to distinguish what is good from what is bad. They define relationships, moral values, sexuality and almost every other aspect of our lives. They set down the patterns for family communication and teach us how we should be with one another. They inspire us to have expectations of ourselves and others. The family beliefs we pick up in childhood influence what we think and how we feel for the rest of our lives.

There are two kinds of beliefs – spoken and unspoken. Spoken beliefs are out in the open and can be discussed. They are the explicit rules that condition children to do what is expected of them. Spoken beliefs teach children what they should, must, ought and have to do. These overtly expressed beliefs are the basis of the rules that condition how we live. They are like computer programs that unconsciously direct behaviour. Often they are disguised as indirect requests or concerned advice.

Spoken beliefs determine our attitudes, judgements, expectations and to a great degree our self-image, whether positive or negative. When children do what is expected of them they meet with approval and learn to feel good. When they go against the wishes of their parents, teachers or church, they meet with disapproval and learn to feel bad. Adults train children by granting or withholding the reward of approval. Many children are so eager to avoid disapproval that they deny or bury their own feelings. They opt to think, feel and act in ways that are likely to generate approval. What was regarded as chaste and virtuous behaviour in the past was often no more than programmed behaviour by teenagers who feared adult sanctions and unmarried pregnancy.

Very young children learn from observation. They absorb their parents' patterns of relating before their critical powers are developed. They acquire behaviours without making a conscious choice. One outcome of this early learning is that if parents have poor relationship skills, children imitate them, and they in their turn are programmed to relate badly. Our family belief system becomes so much a part of us that we fail to recognise how much of our behaviour is conditioned or programmed by others.

For example, parents who believe in the sacredness of marriage may inculcate such a strong belief that 'Marriage is for better or worse' that a daughter might feel she has to remain in a violent marriage. Fortunately the increasing openness in our society regarding family violence may cause her to re-examine that belief. Because it is a spoken belief it is out in the open and can be re-examined and questioned. Once she understands that her behaviour is conditioned by a belief she is free to question, she may ask, 'Why should I remain with this man?' She then becomes open to other possible courses of action. Another belief about the sacredness of respecting human life may challenge her to reconsider remaining 'for better or worse'. She may decide that leaving home to protect her own wellbeing is a greater good than staying and risking serious injury.

UNSPOKEN BELIEFS

It is not quite so simple to reject a belief that you do not know you have. We are all affected by unspoken beliefs which are far more insidious than spoken beliefs because they exist below the level of awareness. They control our behaviour without our being conscious of their existence. For example, if a child picks up a sense of parental discomfort with sexual issues he may assume that sex is a taboo subject not to be mentioned or spoken about in the family.

Children pick up unspoken beliefs and assumptions without parents being conscious of what is happening.

These affect their attitudes to life, relationships and God. Because they are implicit and not spoken about, they are very difficult to correct when they are distorted or wrong. Beliefs are insidious when they are based on wrong information. They create unhealthy expectations that give rise to a distorted way of understanding life, love and spirituality.

HONOUR THY FATHER AND THY MOTHER

Let's take an example. Almost every culture and religion teaches children to 'honour thy father and thy mother'. Of course this is right and proper when parents act in responsible ways. Unfortunately not all parents do. During the 1950s Dr J. Cafe, a distinguished paediatric radiologist in the United States, alerted childcare professionals to non-accidental injuries in infants. When there was no evidence of disease causing fractures in the young children he examined, he came to the conclusion that these injuries were inflicted by parents or childcarers.

The American Humane Society conducted a national survey of maltreated children and found that the physical abuse of children was a national problem. The fact that non-accidental injury occurred could not be denied, and the widespread assumption that it happened as a consequence of poverty or lack of education was disproved by Dr Henry Kempe, who coined the term 'battered baby'. He found abusive parents in all strata of society. He argued that they were people who were 'immature, impulsive, self-centred, hypersensitive and quick to react with poorly controlled aggression'.

The publicity surrounding the death of Maria Colwell

in Britain brought the physical abuse of children into the public forum in the 1970s. The explicit belief that a parent who 'spared the rod' spoiled the child was common. Implicit in this belief was an approval of the practice of disciplining children with physical punishment. Religious beliefs mirrored this acceptance of harsh treatment. God punished with eternal damnation in the fires of hell. Awareness of the damage that was done to children by severe parenting changed the attitudes of society on both sides of the Atlantic to the use of physical punishment to discipline children.

Evidence of the extent of child sexual abuse surfaced in the 1980s and 1990s. It is hardly surprising that the emotional abuse of children, which is so damaging to a child's spirit, has never received the same public attention. Society has not reached the level of maturity where it can be openly acknowledged that most parents hurt children emotionally. Of course they do not do this deliberately. It is the most natural thing in the world for parents to treat children as their parents treated them. Without being aware of what they are doing, adults repeat hurtful patterns of behaviour. The best-intentioned loving parents get things wrong. It is not uncommon for parents unknowingly to undermine the self-esteem and self-confidence of children. In an effort to get a girl or boy to perform well, some adults demand such high standards that they push a child too far. Their efforts to encourage a better performance are counterproductive. For some children who are pushed to achieve, their whole sense of self-worth is tied up in achieving the success their parents desire.

The perfect family

It would be foolish if not irresponsible to pretend that all children live in happy families. The perfect family is a myth. There are no perfect families and there are no perfect children. Some parents behave badly; they neglect or abuse each other and do not care for their children properly. Other families bend over backwards to deny family problems and keep them hidden. If Dad drinks more than is good for him and Mum covers up and acts as if everything is fine, the children are likely to suffer lifelong damage.

The charade of playing Happy Families is very common where alcoholism is a problem. It is terribly damaging for a child. He grows up confused and unable to trust his own experiences. When a parent is in denial about a family problem the child picks up the implicit belief that you must deny reality. The unspoken rule is that: 'You must always act as if everything is fine and never let on that Dad's drinking has the family in chaos.' Children's expectations of being loved by God are powerfully influenced by their experience of being loved in the family. Youngsters, in a sense, deify their parents. If Mum and Dad are loving and dependable, that will be the image of God the child has. If the child's parents cannot be trusted and let him down, it is difficult for him to expect God to be any different.

Wrong assumptions

It can be fascinating to uncover the implicit beliefs that form your family's attitudes to love, life, sex and religion. Some of these unstated beliefs can be highly amusing and unexpected. It is so easy for a child to misunderstand what he sees or hears and make a totally wrong assumption. If incorrect assumptions are not corrected they become beliefs that influence behaviour. Let me give you an example of how easily this can happen.

When one of my daughters was about six years of age I had some women neighbours in for coffee. I had forgotten to put a sugar bowl on the table. One of my friends asked for sugar. My daughter was playing in the room and I asked her to help. She looked at my friend, amazed, and said, 'I didn't know women used sugar.'

When we listed the family and friends who regularly had tea or coffee with us it transpired that none of our usual women visitors used sugar. Many of the men did. My daughter assumed that only men took sugar. She made a logical assumption that was wrong because it was based on too narrow a range of people. The consequences of that error would not have been serious if she had never found out. However, it shows how easily children can pick up distorted ideas without adults having any awareness that there is a problem.

RELIGION AND SPIRITUALITY

Most people are aware that parental attitudes to God have a strong bearing on children's attitudes to religion and spirituality. In earlier chapters we saw that the couple relationship of parents plays an important role in influencing how their children understand sexual responsibility. It is important for parents to be aware of how influential family beliefs are in the matter of the adolescent's valuing of himself as a person. Good self-esteem is closely allied with feeling loved and accepted just because you are who you are.

All the great spiritualities begin with who we are and how we are. One of the most gifted spiritual guides of the twentieth century defined spirituality as 'that which brings one to inner transformation'. Anthony de Mello challenged people to wake up to the way their thinking was programmed and conditioned. He said, 'Spirituality is the most practical thing in the whole wide world. I challenge anyone to think of anything more practical than spirituality as I have defined it – not piety, not devotion, not religion, not worship, but spirituality – waking up, waking up.'

Many teenagers who no longer go to church are waking up. Unhappy with the Sunday liturgies that leave them uninspired and unmoved, they have turned their back on the institutional church. Many parents worry that young people who have stopped attending church have lost their religion. This is simply not true. They remain beautiful, spiritual young people. It is healthy to have a questioning faith. Examining religious beliefs is as important for teenagers as exploring their family values. Some come to a new understanding that strengthens their faith. Others walk away from institutional religion, but this does not necessarily mean that they turn their back on their own spirituality.

Religion means far more than worshipping in a community of believers. It has to do with our understanding of life. Ideally, religious practice would lead to spirituality, to that self-awakening that is essential for inner transformation and spiritual growth. Sadly it frequently does not, and disillusioned young people look elsewhere to meet their spiritual needs. They find God in nature, in loving relationships, in meditation and in the religious practices of the East.

SPIRITUAL EXPERIENCES

Spiritual experiences bring people into the presence of mystery in life. Ideally an appreciation of nature and its beauty would move us to an appreciation of the creator of such beauty. In spiritual experiences people transcend self, and something deep within them is touched. Making love has the potential to be one of the most beautiful of shared spiritual experiences. The experience of two becoming one is both sacred and holy. It is a transcendent experience which touches the deepest part of the self. We can call this the soul.

Ideally, religious beliefs and practices would lead to spiritual development. Sadly, religious beliefs have proved an impediment to a fulfilled sexual relationship for many good people. It cannot be denied that generations of Christians were taught to feel guilty for taking pleasure in sex, even within a marriage that was blessed. Poorly understood church rules served to alienate people from their deepest experiences of intimacy. Many couples never enjoyed the freedom to experience the pleasure of intercourse as truly holy and blessed by God. They were never educated to recognise the sacredness of sexual intimacy. Both sexuality and spirituality flow from a sacred place, the life-giving spring that is within each person.

RELIGION IS NOT OPPOSED TO SEX

There are many different theologies of sexuality that can help people appreciate sex in a positive way. Despite what many good Christians believe, religion is not opposed to sexuality. All world religions are opposed to sexuality *as it is misused.* It is worth noting that the Old Testament account of how God created woman is not associated with procreation.

In the Book of Genesis God said, 'It is not good that man be alone. I will make him a helpmate.' Woman, a sexually different person, was created. God so loved humankind that Eve was created and given as a companion to Adam so that man would no longer be alone. Woman was created as a partner for man. Sexuality is God's gift. It enables woman and man to become one, to unite in love. Adam and Eve were naked in the garden and they were comfortable in their nakedness. There is no inference that they should be ashamed or embarrassed.

SEXUAL OPENNESS IN THE BIBLE

The Bible celebrates erotic love in the best possible way. Among Christians the sexual union of two lovers is understood as a symbol for the relationship between Christ and his Church. The Jewish rabbis similarly used the intimate relationship between lovers to symbolise the relationship between Yahweh and Israel. The account of the passionate relationship between the lovers in the Song of Songs is positive and beautiful. The love that is celebrated is ardent, erotic and holy. The sensuousness of erotic love is fully appreciated and celebrated. The intensity of feelings is expressed in extravagant language that celebrates the voluptuous seductiveness of the human body from head to toe.

The writer is obviously sexually experienced. There is a clear understanding of the exclusiveness of the relationship celebrated: 'My beloved is mine and I am his.' The flowery language brings out the intensity of the physical desire the couple enjoy. They delight in being together:

> How beautiful you are, how charming, my love, my
>   delight!
> In stature like the palm tree,
> 'I will climb the palm tree,' I resolved,
> 'I will seize its clusters of dates.'
> May your breasts be clusters of grapes,
> your breath sweet-scented as apples,
> your speaking, superlative wine.
>
> Song of Songs 7: 8-10

Here love is sexually expressed in the context of an ongoing relationship. There is obviously an expectation of commitment. I suspect that many parents would be aghast at the idea that teenagers might enjoy this explicit biblical account of the lovers. Others might want young people to be educated to appreciate the high regard for the spirituality of sexuality that is evident in the Scriptures. Yet others might be somewhat concerned, worried about the effect of such an erotic account of sexual love.

 EROTIC IMAGERY

It is understandable that many parents would be shocked at the idea of exposing teenagers to the imagery in the

Song of Songs. Some might even consider it harmful. Expert opinion is divided regarding adult storylines in television programmes which make children acutely aware of sexual matters. Many professionals believe that erotica is a harmless sexual outlet; yet studies show that a frequent diet of erotic sexual material may ascribe an unrealistic importance to sex.

Parents cannot protect young people from seeing sexual pictures that titillate. They can, however, do something to ensure that reasons for delaying sexual activity are presented in a way that makes sense to intelligent young people whose hormones are in overdrive. It cannot be denied that sex is a powerful drive. Young people are naturally curious about what it feels like. They have to be educated to understand that sex is a way of communicating at a very deep level. They need to understand that there are positive consequences to conserving sexual energy and channelling it in other ways. If a couple cannot talk openly and sincerely about everyday things, how can they expect to communicate at a sexual level? Good communication is necessary for good sex. Deferring sexual activity requires the discipline of delaying gratification. Young men must be educated about the differences in sexual responsiveness between men and women. They would benefit from appreciating the skill involved in being responsive lovers who can delay their own pleasure. The kind of self-control that is needed to heighten anticipation and allow sexual passion and excitement to build to a wonderfully intense climax needs to be valued. Some married couples could benefit from practising these skills too. There is an old joke that foreplay begins for a wife at six o'clock in the evening and at half past eleven for her husband. Couples would benefit from knowing that their expectation while waiting allows excitement to build up. This increases the intensity of their sexual experience.

DOUBLE STANDARDS – INFLUENCE OF ADVERTISEMENTS

Society implicitly promises teenagers that sex is the ticket to adulthood but fails to ensure that they are sexually educated. Commercial interests encourage adolescent girls to dress in tight, figure-hugging clothes that make them sexually alluring. It is hypocritical of parents to ignore the sexually stimulating imagery that encourages teenagers to behave in adult ways. Advertisements influence young people's perception of which products they should use and of how to dress and act in a way that is attractive to the opposite sex. The implicit belief that one must behave in a sexy way to attract boys is widely accepted by young girls. Ideas that everyone shares – or at least that no one contradicts – are likely to be accepted as true.

Many adults claim to have strong views on sexual morality yet ignore the spirituality of sexuality. This is understandable. Before the sexual revolution of the 1960s it was considered indelicate or improper for a couple contemplating marriage to educate themselves about having good sex. Many families have never recovered from that erroneous understanding of sexual morality. Many adults feel an underlying guilt about nudity and fail to have any aesthetic appreciation of the erotic images portrayed in literature and the visual arts.

118

This confusion about sexual morality makes it difficult for adults to answer adolescents' questions about acceptable sexual behaviour. There is no doubt that traditional church teaching on sexuality has been silently eroded by changing attitudes to sex in society. In the very recent past an overemphasis on sexual sin had the damaging effect of encouraging married couples to repress their sexual feelings. Some healthy, sexually active couples learned to feel guilty about enjoying sexual pleasure, even within the intimacy of marriage. A few deliberately repressed their sensual and erotic feelings in the misguided belief that this was what God wanted of them.

The long-term damage that has occurred in Christian families because of this negative focus on sexuality haunts Western society. In the measure that people try to deny, ignore or repress their sexuality, they repress their energy for relating to and loving others. Today, more than ever before, parents and teachers need to teach young people about sexuality in a way that affirms the value of physical affection for loving people. Whether a person is young or old, married, single or celibate, he or she has intimacy needs that cannot be ignored.

SEXUAL PEOPLE

We are all sexual persons. Our femininity or masculinity, that is our sexuality, shapes our capacity to relate to others. A proper appreciation of the old-fashioned virtue of chastity brings together the sexual and the spiritual. Fr Donald Goergan OP says: 'A chaste person is a sexual person and is in fact a supreme exemplification of what it means to be sexual.' Chastity is positive about affectionate touches, sexual feelings, sexual desires and sexual experiences. Sadly, poor religious teaching in the past tried to impose a distorted chastity on people by making them repress and deny their sexual feelings. Whole generations suffered guilt because they were implicitly taught that sexual feelings were sinful.

It would be unfair to point the finger at religious teaching alone. The puritanical attitudes to sex that created so much unhealthy repression came from a blend of religious, social and political beliefs. When family wealth was inherited through the male line it was necessary to ensure pure-bred sons. To keep the family blood lines unadulterated it was essential that the woman who bore the male heir was a virgin. Society used negative attitudes to sex as a social control to protect family inheritance rights. Sexual expression was permitted for the purposes of procreation within marriage. Male virginity was never prized in the same way as female virginity. Although chastity is still valued in religious teaching, it is no longer highly prized in a secular society.

Many of the young people I work with in schools are puzzled by what they see as the hypocrisy and deceit of adult attitudes to sex and sexuality. They question the double standards of sexual morality by which women and men are treated differently. They rightly reject the dual standard that condemns in women behaviour that is condoned in men. They challenge public figures who demand one standard of behaviour in public while privately practising a different standard.

Motives for sexual abstinence

Teenage attitudes to sexual morality are bound up with
family attitudes, religious teaching, the influence of
society and peer pressure. There is a great need to
contradict the negative attitudes that preventive teaching
about pregnancy and sexually transmitted disease has
given girls and boys. God made females and males
differently and these differences make them sexually
attractive to one another all through life. Sexual attraction
is part of the divine plan to draw women and men
together in different kinds of friendship. It is not meant
to be repressed. It is meant to be experienced and
enjoyed.

Jesus never taught that sexual abstinence is superior to
sexual intimacy within an exclusive committed relationship.
This is church teaching. In the early medieval church
married people were counselled to practise sexual abstinence during the seasons of fasting. One could understand the injunction to refrain from sex when couples had
no control over fertility. In some extreme cases abstinence
was encouraged on Thursdays in memory of Christ's
arrest, on Fridays in memory of His death, on Saturdays
in memory of the Virgin Mary, on Sundays in honour of
the resurrection and on Mondays in commemoration of
the departed. There is little evidence to show how closely
this advice was followed by couples. Many theologians
were opposed to such exacting requirements.

Before the Second Vatican Council that ended in 1965
Catholics were taught that God allowed sexual intercourse
within marriage only for procreation. To have sex for any
other reason was concupiscent. In the moral climate of

the 1950s and early 1960s it was not uncommon for teenage girls to be unprepared for menstruation. Adults were so focused on keeping young people innocent that they avoided preparing them properly for puberty. Some couples who got married were uninstructed in the facts of life and unappreciative of the beauty and sacredness of sexuality. Conscientiously chaste couples who entered marriage unprepared for a sexual relationship were often ignorant of the realities of childbirth. There is no point in blaming any person or institution for what happened. People did their best in the climate of the times.

It is hardly surprising that the spirituality of sexuality was not understood by people who were taught to deny the graced experience of sexual union. The strict puritanical teaching of the Christian churches on sexual morality encouraged rigid and unbending attitudes. By the 1970s many Catholics publicly questioned the Vatican ban on artificial means of family planning. It was seen as inflexible and devoid of compassion. There is no doubt that this teaching has alienated lay people and done much more damage than the sexual scandals of the 1990s to the authority of the Church to teach on sexual matters. Surely it is inevitable that a dictum that demands blind obedience will be discarded as irrelevant when it is found to interfere with the quality of the lives of people of good faith.

CONFUSION ABOUT INTIMACY

It is very probable that what many people were taught to regard as the sexual sin of lust did not stem from lechery but from insecurity and fear and the natural need for the body to be touched affectionately. Denying, ignoring or repressing feelings does not lead to spiritual growth but to an unhealthy preoccupation with suppressing what is unacceptable. This makes it more likely that the unwanted behaviour will recur. What is repressed will leak out or reappear in a disguised form.

Many adults were mystified when they were teenagers by the teaching that sexual pleasure was good under one set of circumstances and bad under another. Sadly confusion regarding bodily touching tainted normal affectionate actions with sexual guilt. Fear of sinning against holy purity engendered a fear of affectionate spontaneity that still inhibits large numbers of adults today. They pass on their inhibitions to children, who sometimes rebel in adolescence and react by going too far in the opposite direction.

Religion that ignored the spirituality of sexuality caused people to feel guilty about sexual sin without helping them understand the motivation behind their own behaviour. Many adults who are parents today grew up in cold and repressed families. In the early 1950s demands for chastity in dress showed very little understanding of this virtue. Catholic women were asked, 'Not to wear clothes less than four inches below the knee, or, so tight-fitting and skimpy as to give undue prominence to the figure, or in any other way bordering on immodesty, such as slit skirts or dispensing with a brassiere, dresses with low backs or a low neck line that exposes the person unnecessarily, thereby offending against modesty.'

Parents were urged to 'withhold their daughters from

taking part in public athletic exercises and gymnastic contests'. Some clergy opposed coeducational schools on the ground that undue familiarity between the sexes was likely to stir sinful curiosity. Women were burdened with the responsibility of being a temptation to men. In one religious publication, unnamed 'responsible' medical doctors were quoted as saying that 'mannish dress for women is positively dangerous to their morals. The apparel known as shorts and slacks, at first only used by the sporting type of woman, leads to a desire to improve on nature. To do so, artificial means are used, and, in turn, these result in over-developed passions that crave self-satisfaction and ultimately cause the loss of control over the lower passions.'

IMPOSED VALUES

It is no wonder that so many parents have implicit beliefs that have conditioned them to feel uncomfortable about sexual pleasure. Although today's adults were older when they fell in love and started dating, they were less likely to experiment sexually than adolescents are today. Most teenagers in the 1970s experienced enormous social and religious pressure to remain chaste. They adhered to strict moral standards and the majority saved sex for marriage. The ideal of the virgin bride was highly valued when society prized chastity. It is probably true to say that the practice of pre-marital chastity owed as much to fear of hell and the consequences of an unwanted pregnancy as to virtue.

If the traditional morals and values of society were truly accepted as a free choice rather than being imposed by fear, the rapid change in sexual behaviour that took place when contraception became freely available would not have happened. Fertility control has changed the attitude of society to pre-marital sex. The availability of contraception has had important repercussions for women of all ages. It has taken away the fear of pregnancy and made it more difficult for women to refuse sex. It has given men the expectation that women are always sexually available. It has challenged people to question their sexual values. For Catholics it raises moral questions about God's plan as to how women and men use their sexuality. The majority do not accept that the papal teaching on family planning is God's will for couples.

Deciding how to deal with sexual feelings and desires is only one part of the process of self-awareness that leads to wholeness. Sex has enormous potential to bring wholeness and healing when properly used, and emotional hurt when misused. Needy people who have sex in the absence of a loving, committed relationship are likely to feel used and wounded. When sexual intimacy is shared by a loving couple there is a sacred dimension to their lovemaking that brings unity and wholeness. The loving intimacy that nourishes affectionate relationships involves the whole person, body, mind and spirit. It is a truly spiritual experience to have the freedom to be open and loving in this holistic way.

8

LIVING WITHOUT SEX

CHANGING ATTITUDES

Parents, teachers and the clergy would be foolish if not irresponsible to deny that radical changes have occurred in the thinking of young people regarding pre-marital sex. Many adolescents do not see any value in saving sex for marriage. Some do not even consider it important to save sex for a relationship where there is a long-term commitment. The modern thinking is: if you love somebody it is OK to have sex. If you decide not to have sex the assumption is that you have a low sex drive, that there is probably something wrong with you. Celibacy is no longer valued as a life-choice. Anyone who chooses to live without sex is treated with suspicion.

This is a worrying change in attitude, especially as most adolescents fall in and out of love with great regularity. I do not know of any research that gives accurate figures for the number of romances either girls or boys enjoy between the time they start dating and the time they finally settle down with a life partner. In my experience it is becoming rarer for a couple who meet as teenagers to stay together. The majority of young people have romances with many different partners before making a commitment. When this happens, a couple are more likely to live together than to get married.

A LOOK AT CELIBACY

Being celibate can be understood as 'not having sex with a partner'. Celibacy also means the choice of consecrated virginity made by religious women and men who take a vow not to marry. Celibate religious are not asexual, as is sometimes mistakenly believed. It is understandable that many people still hold the wrong idea that celibate chastity is based on anti-sexual asceticism or emotional repression. It is not. Celibate people fall in love and experience sexual attraction. They make a choice not to act on those feelings. They choose to forego an exclusive relationship and to express affectionate feelings in non-genital ways. The value of this kind of celibacy is under scrutiny from both within and without religious communities.

Unfortunately, sexual scandals among a tiny minority of men in religious life who sexually abused children has given celibacy a bad press. The fear that it leads to paedophilia is widespread, even though it is known that paedophilia is a serious mental illness. Research evidence shows that the majority of paedophiles are married men, many of whose marriages have broken down. Only a tiny minority are clerics.

In the past a higher standard of morality was expected from all clergymen. Protestant ministers were allowed to marry, but Roman Catholic priests were not. Catholics were taught that God valued consecrated celibacy above marriage. The overemphasis on sexual sins made people anxious about enjoying sensual pleasures, even when they were married. Some couples deliberately repressed their sexual and erotic feelings in the misguided belief that to take pleasure in sex made them guilty of concupiscence.

The long-term damage that has occurred because of this negative focus on sexuality haunts both Christian families and religious communities. The suspicion that attached to normal loving friendships between celibate people in convents and seminaries made it impossible for many religious to integrate their sexuality and spirituality. Some religious orders failed celibate women and men when they encouraged them to distrust human affection.

A SUPERIOR STATE OF LIFE?

The suggestion that one can be both sexual and spiritual is still not widely accepted. Many religious people who chose a celibate lifestyle in the past genuinely believed that it was superior to both the married and the single states of life. It is sad that many celibate people cut themselves off emotionally because they were implicitly taught to deny that they had sexual feelings, desires and needs just like everybody else. Many who did became cold and aloof, unable to reach out to people with love. In a misguided desire to live up to their vocation, they isolated themselves and became lonely and bitter people in the process.

Celibacy is a charism or gift of relationship that allows celibate religious the freedom to go out in love and friendship to all. When religious sisters, brothers and priests are warm human beings, they demonstrate that one can lead a happy and fulfilled life as a celibate person. Many school chaplains and youth leaders are looked up to by young people. Those who are in touch with their feelings and have the freedom to meet their emotional needs have a lot to offer them.

In our modern society single people who choose not to marry are made to feel defensive about their single status. They are often viewed with suspicion. It is vital to contradict the popularly held notion that all single people are on the lookout for a partner. The perception that all single women are out to steal husbands or seduce defenceless youths is widely held by other women. It could not be more wrong. The male assumption that single women are easy to 'hit on' also needs to be contradicted. This will be easier to do if young people fully understand that celibacy, or choosing to live without sex, has benefits that make it worth considering.

The myths young people accept about the need for sex and the harm they believe is done to celibate people by sexual frustration will not be contradicted by accurate information alone. Teenagers need role models who are capable of intimacy and who have the freedom to enjoy warm, intimate, physically affectionate, chaste relationships *without being genitally sexually active.*

SEXUAL FRUSTRATION IS A FACT OF LIFE

It would help if parents acknowledged that they have a sexual dimension to their lives and that they sometimes have to deal with sexual frustration. It would also benefit teenagers to be challenged to think about the thousands of adults who are not in a couple relationship. Most of them survive beautifully. Sexual abstinence is a fact of life for single, celibate and some married people. It is seldom openly discussed. In real life couples' relationships do break up. Happily married people sometimes have celibacy thrust on them. Perhaps a spouse has to go away for a few months' training. A partner may be sent abroad on business or the couple may be involuntarily separated when one party is incarcerated in gaol. Every day people who have been used to sexual intimacy are put in the position of living without sex.

Increasing numbers of married people admit that they neglect the sexual side of their relationship and effectively live celibate lives. Genital sex plays only a small part in what it means to be a sexual person. Teenagers need to be aware that learning to deal appropriately with sexual feelings and desires is one of the tasks of adolescence. Young people who fail to develop the discipline to defer gratification will not make either sensitive or caring lovers.

People who choose to live celibate lives for religious reasons learn to differentiate between affective and genital sexuality. They learn to enjoy warm, intimate friendships that do not involve genital activity. There is a richness to platonic friendships that do not involve sexual intimacy. Teenagers who do not experience such friendships are missing out.

Sexual openness

The failure of Irish families to discuss sexual issues in an open and honest way is indicative of a discomfort with sexuality. This leaves many adolescents dependent on their peers for guidance about appropriate dating behaviour. Some are lucky enough to enjoy ongoing, supportive, platonic friendships. Sadly those who have poor self-esteem are more likely to look for affection in sexual ways. For teenage girls sexual intimacy intensifies emotional involvement. For boys it sometimes completes a conquest. Males tend to separate sex from love, and some men have no reservations about abandoning their conquests.

Single people who choose to save sex for marriage have a lot to offer young people. They have different expectations of relationships. They have probably found helpful ways of dealing with sexual desires and frustrations. They understand that feelings of sexual attraction are natural and they can deal with them in ways that lead to intimacy. They can offer suggestions that will not be found on the problem pages of the magazines that sexually educate many adolescents. Having sex is potentially a life-changing decision that is often taken too lightly.

Many adults who are parents today never learned to feel comfortable about their own sexuality. They grew up with a negative attitude to sex and sexuality and now find themselves in a dilemma. They are caught between the traditional and liberal views of sex. The traditional approach is negative about touch, sexual feelings, sexual desires and sensual experiences. The liberal view is that you cannot stop young people having sex – all you can do is teach them how to protect themselves.

For many middle of the road parents, neither of these

approaches is an acceptable option. Aware that young people in love have incredibly intense emotional feelings, they want to find a way to encourage them to delay sexual activity. Yet they do not want to scare them into repressing their sexual feelings and desires as previous generations were frightened into doing. Parents seldom realise how difficult it is for teenagers in love to cope with their powerful sexual feelings. They need guidance and help if they are to make sexually responsible choices. It will not be easy for adults to assist, because it involves an honest look at their own sexual values. It also entails a thorough scrutiny of the messages about relationships and sexuality their offspring picked up as young children.

A POSITIVE APPROACH

Parents who want to educate young people to delay sex should expect tough questions about their own sexual values and behaviour. The first and most obvious question adolescents ask is: 'Why save sex for marriage?' I suspect that many adults faced with this question would immediately give either of two answers. The more traditional parents might say, 'Because sex before marriage is a sin.' Other parents might respond with, 'Because I don't want you to be a party to a teenage pregnancy or contract AIDS.'

Both these answers have a negative focus – sin, pregnancy and disease. This approach smacks of disapproval and fear, the old approach that successfully discouraged young people until contraception changed both attitudes and rules. Behaviour that is kept in place by fear changes when the fear is taken away. Surely it is time to move on from those negative reasons for delaying sexual intimacy and give young people a more positive, holistic approach to sexuality. Sex involves the whole person, body, mind and spirit. Today, more than ever before, parents and teachers need to teach young people about sexuality in a way that affirms the value of meeting their affectionate needs in respectful relationships.

It is widely accepted that a good deal of sexual experimentation is a vain attempt by young people to find in sex the love and reassurance they miss out on in the family. When a couple has sex the relationship changes. Even pre-pubescent children understand this. Eleven and twelve-year-old girls and boys can explain that they would not kiss the girl or boy next door. 'You wouldn't be friends in the same way after getting off.' This is the slang term for intimate kissing, known as French kissing to adults and 'getting off', 'snogging' or 'tonsil hockey' to children.

EDUCATION CHOICES

Young people strongly desire sex. Parents have choices about whether they educate them to understand the physical, emotional and spiritual consequences of acting on these desires. Until very recently the majority of parents with religious beliefs left this task to the clergy. Since some Catholics rejected Vatican teaching on family planning, the power of that church to control the sexual behaviour of couples both within and outside marriage has been diminished.

The control of fertility has radically changed attitudes to pre-marital sex. Teenagers of all denominations are dismissive of church teaching, though the churches still retain some influence, particularly in schools and parishes where young people look up to chaplains, teachers or youth leaders.

Parents are naturally worried about the value-free advice adolescents get from the media and their peers. If young people believe that all their friends are having sex they will probably feel a pressure to have it too – and often for all the wrong reasons. It is up to parents who want them to wait to encourage them to think more positively about choosing not to get sexually enmeshed in couple relationships. They should be given factual information that will reassure them of the positive advantages of living without the complications of a sexually intimate relationship.

RELATING AS SEXUAL PEOPLE

A good place to begin is by explaining that women and men relate to each other as sexual people. In so far as people try to deny, ignore or repress their sexuality, they repress their energy for relating to and loving others. Our sexuality, that is our femininity or our masculinity, shapes our capacity to relate to others. Our ability to go out in love depends on our capacity to find out how to live our sexuality – our relational capacity – in ways that are both personally fulfilling, and energising or lifegiving for others.

Our ability to love others, whether we are talking about loving a special friend, our family, our neighbours or our God, rests on our capacity for human intimacy. Young people need to be educated about the important role of affectionate intimacy in the healthy wellbeing of the human person, whether married, celibate or single. They need to understand that women and men can love each other very much and choose not to have sex.

Surely we owe it to teenagers to help them understand how they are influenced by the pressure to be sexual that is coming at them from their own powerful desires, their peers, the print media and the television programmes and videos they watch.

TEENAGE MISINFORMATION

It is fascinating to listen to teenagers talk about what the Christian churches teach. The majority are aware that organised religions forbid sex before marriage. Very few respect or agree with this teaching. These are some typical comments from young teenagers:

- 'The church says it is against religion to have sex before marriage. Joseph thought Mary did it with another fella when they were engaged and he was going to divorce her.'
- 'The church says no to sex before marriage. We don't know why.'
- 'Priests say sex before marriage is a sin. It's stupid they don't talk or do anything about it. Maybe they are too embarrassed or don't have enough education. We should make up our own minds.'
- 'The church says you shouldn't have sex before marriage to avoid unwanted pregnancies. We think it is a mortal sin that they disapprove of contraception. It's breaking the commandment, "Thou shall not kill." Condoms should be acceptable because there are a lot of lethal diseases nowadays.'

It is hardly a surprise that young people do not agree with their church's view on sex before marriage. The majority of Catholic parents have reservations on aspects of church teaching too. They do not accept their church's ban on family planning. Today the use of contraception is general in Catholic countries worldwide. Parents have decided that God does not intend every act of sexual intercourse to be procreative. This generation has taken matters a step further and asked the obvious question: 'If this is so, why should sex be restricted to marriage?'

WHY SAVE SEX FOR MARRIAGE?

There is no easy answer. The morality of an action is not judged in isolation. The intention behind the action is also a factor in deciding what is moral, immoral or amoral. Adolescents who debate the issue among themselves are deeply influenced by their parents' values. If the parents' reasons for avoiding pre-marital sex are fears of an unwanted pregnancy or STDs they know how to assuage these worries. Use contraception and the problem is solved.

Most teenagers are curious about what sex feels like. If they are in a relationship their focus is mostly on the physical, bodily aspects of intimacy. When they think of the consequences of having sex they seldom look beyond the possibility of infection or pregnancy. They seldom think of the emotional or spiritual consequences. They are not to blame for this. Adolescents will not learn to have a holistic attitude by osmosis. They must be taught, and this necessary instruction should take place in a safe, non-judgemental environment where they have the freedom to examine and explore their own attitudes and values.

CONFUSING LUST AND INTIMACY NEEDS

Good sex education needs to be relevant to the life experiences of young people. It is pointless for parents to demand that teenagers remain celibate. It would be preferable to help them understand how easily their lust needs can be mistaken for intimacy needs. I suspect that most parents and very many teachers need to be sexually educated themselves before they are ready to discuss the difference between one's affectionate and genital needs.

It is seldom acknowledged that sex education is a lifelong process. Parents need to listen to adolescents, who are frequently better informed than adults. Some have questions about sexual morality that most adults cannot answer. Since this is true, the wise parent will admit, 'I never thought about that. I have no idea. Tell me what *you* think.' Since teenagers query the value of marriage and celibacy they have some interesting ideas to contribute to the debate. Perhaps religious people could broaden the debate to explore what chastity means for people in different life situations in the modern world.

FIRST SEX

For many teenage couples first sex is an unplanned event. It just happens in the heat of the moment and is seldom a memorable experience. It is a thirty-second wonder for him and a disappointment for her. The Kinsey report showed that a woman's ability to achieve orgasm increases in direct relation to the length of the relationship. An American survey among college students who had sex showed that the majority of women and about 25 per cent of the men surveyed wished they had waited. Tender, honest, emotionally intimate, erotic sex is best within an exclusive, committed relationship.

ANOTHER OPTION

Affectionate relationships help couples develop an appreciation of the intimate communication that occurs when sex does not get in the way. For women, talking makes for closeness. The intimate bonding that occurs for them during ordinary conversations is very important. It is as if they first need to bare their souls before they are ready to bare their bodies.

If parents can educate teenage girls and boys to take a more holistic approach to sex, they will learn a different way of understanding their sexual needs. They will have different expectations of relationships too. They may come to appreciate that living without sex is a favourable option. Some may even value celibacy as a difficult but worthwhile experience. Many people might benefit from knowing that not alone does abstinence make the heart grow fonder, it can also lead to the development of the good communication that makes for really great sex. What better motivation could you find to encourage sexually mature young people to develop good communication skills?

9

HOW EFFECTIVE IS SEX EDUCATION?

There is little reason to believe that it is easier for
teachers to give information on sex than it is for parents.
Many teachers admit this. Discomfiture at teaching
children about relationships and sexuality is common.
Embarrassment about sex education appears to be a uni-
versal problem for people on both sides of the Atlantic.
American parents believe that children in Europe learn
about sex in as matter-of-fact a manner as they learn
about brushing their teeth. People living in Europe are
only too well aware that they do not.

In Britain, Ireland and America children are growing
up without being adequately educated about relationships
and sexuality. One has only to look at the statistics for
teenage pregnancy and the spread of STDs to see that
teenage promiscuity is a global problem. It has serious
consequences for family life and for society. American
research shows that school-based sex education programmes that are value-free have not proved effective in
reducing the numbers of teenage pregnancies.

Britain has the highest unmarried teenage pregnancy rate

in Europe. Irish children are more likely to experiment with sex at an early age than their American counterparts. According to a survey carried out by Colman Duggan, a senior social worker at the sexual assault unit in Our Lady's Hospital for Sick Children in Dublin, and Toni Cavanagh-Jones, an American academic, the childhood sexual experiences of adolescents in the two countries are very similar. 59 per cent of Irish students and 57 per cent of Americans believed it was normal for children under twelve to have some kind of sexual experience.

There is no doubt that pre-pubescent children have an enormous amount of information about sex, contraception and abortion. Sadly this information is mostly value-free. If such information is not put into a moral or spiritual framework, hurtful, disrespectful attitudes to sex will not be contradicted and challenged. Many parents admit that they do not have the expertise to deal adequately with sex education. They want schools to take over the task. Some parents, on the other hand, are against school-based programmes and prefer to educate children at home. I think there is a role here for both parents and teachers. Some teachers may find it easier to teach about the physical aspect of sex than about its emotional or spiritual aspects. There are certain difficulties in dealing realistically with the emotional and spiritual dimensions of a subject that touches people's lives so intimately. Children come from different family situations. Their parents may have different ideas about what they feel it is appropriate for children to know at different ages. Teaching sex education is different from teaching academic subjects, because children's family backgrounds must be taken into account.

The unhealthily negative attitudes that some children pick up from their parents, that sex is harmful, dirty or shameful, need to be contradicted. It is unrealistic to put the onus on teachers alone. Young people need to be taught that women and men relate to each other as sexual people. Many parents would quarrel with this language because they have too narrow a view of sexuality, a view shared by some educators. They will claim that children at puberty have no need to know more than the basic facts. Out of a misguided protectiveness some parents and teachers cling to the notion of childhood innocence. Not alone do they fail to provide timely or accurate information, but they strongly discourage children from asking necessary questions or being honest about their sexual curiosity.

EMBARRASSMENT

Ideally, sharing information about something that is meant to be sacred and beautiful should be a happy and pleasant experience. Yet many people who are put in the position of giving sex education become anxious and fraught. It is strange that so many otherwise intelligent people take it for granted that giving sex education will evoke embarrassment and trepidation. These negative reactions are probably caused by the residue of guilt so many people still carry regarding concupiscence. The ugly shadow of using others for personal sexual pleasure (the definition of concupiscence) darkens what should be a joyful sharing of information about the joys of sexual love. The healthy development of a sexual identity includes the physical, emotional and spiritual dimensions of a person's experience.

It is a natural part of growing up for children to be curious about what sex is like and to discuss it with each other. Much of what they share is expressed in a vulgar and crude fashion. If their parents are not able to discuss these matters with them, as many are not, they are likely to accept the information they get from their peers as accurate and true. Wrong information that groups of young people share is likely to be accepted as fact, unless challenged by adults.

BREAKING TABOOS

Almost all children pursue their own sex education during adolescence. They make sure that adults are not around when they go scouring novels, magazines and medical books for salacious tit-bits about what sex is like. The fact that the information they get from these sources – and from television and videos – is often crude and sometimes perverted should not be ignored. If adults are serious about teaching young people about the loving, respectful attitudes to others that lead to genuine sexual freedom, a more positive appreciation of sexuality is needed. The taboos that keep families silent and children poorly informed must be broken.

The earlier children mature physically, the more important it is to ensure that parents and teachers are alerted to the sources of their sexual information. In any serious effort to give young people effective relationships and sexuality education it must be admitted that marital problems exist between couples. It is important to teach about two-parent families where parents are married to each other. It is equally important to recognise the other family situations in which pupils may find themselves. These must not be denied, ignored, or indeed, denigrated.

It cannot be denied that disrespectful attitudes to sex are learned in the family as well as from peers. Dysfunctional patterns of behaviour are passed down from parents to children. Girls and boys who come from troubled families must be educated to understand that they have choices. They can choose to have the same kind of relationship as their parents or they can make a conscious decision to develop a different kind. Effective relationships and sexuality education has the potential to teach communication skills and change teenagers' attitudes to relationships. It can help them have more realistic expectations of falling in love and show them the need to work at sustaining loving, nurturing relationships.

CONSULTATION BETWEEN HOME AND SCHOOL

There is a need for consultation between parents and teachers when schools undertake Relationships and Sexuality Education (RSE) programmes. While any such programme must teach young people about the ideals of marriage it must also deal with the reality of children's family experiences. It is vital that no child is ever made to feel that his family situation is unacceptable. Many teachers find that the wisdom of Solomon is needed if they are to communicate sound moral values sensitively to children who come from irregular family situations. When the parents of children in a class have contradictory attitudes to pre-marital sex and have different moral values, the teacher is put in a very difficult position.

This is the reality in many classrooms. It is vitally important for parents to ensure that schools have an open policy on answering the questions children ask in RSE class. In some schools there is a closed policy. This means that a child is only allowed to ask the teacher questions on the material covered in any lesson. Children are warned that no other questions will be considered. If a child asks an 'extra-curricular' question the teacher may refer the question to a parent. This approach is favoured by many teachers because it protects them from the ire of parents who might complain about a child getting inappropriate information. It also saves them from having to deal with embarrassing classroom situations.

It is, however, potentially disastrous for the students. Closed RSE teaching leaves them with unanswered questions. If a child feels, as many do, that he cannot talk to his parents, he is left ignorant, at the mercy of equally ill-informed peers who will probably offer inaccurate and value-free information. Parents and teachers who refuse to answer children's questions about sex, or who avoid answering such questions, are failing them. No responsible adult would allow an untrained twelve-year-old sex educator to instruct pupils in the classroom. Teachers who suggest that they are protecting the interests of more innocent children when they decline to reply to a precocious child are effectively empowering juvenile sex educators to teach in the playground. It is hardly realistic to think that the other children in the class who heard the question will ignore it. Once their appetite for information has been whetted they will leave no stone unturned

until they find an answer. The first child to find information immediately tells his friends, and the result is
surely counter to the whole purpose of RSE.

It is true that some children set up a teacher by asking
embarrassing questions. If the teacher is not prepared to
deal with the question in class, the child who asked the
question has an increased standing in the eyes of the peer
group. Being 'in the know' confers on the child a status
that is envied. A surprising number of children assume
that teachers who refuse to answer questions are either
embarrassed or scared. They often protect them from
further embarrassment and simply stop asking questions
in class.

OPEN TEACHING

In schools where there is an open policy children know
that their questions will be answered. When they use
'street language' the teacher gives them the correct terms.
She usually invites them to ask the questions again using
the correct terminology. In her answer she gently corrects
wrong information or unacceptable attitudes: 'I can
understand you using those words, but could you ask the
question again using more grown-up language?' or 'I find
that offensive to me as a woman. Would you try saying it
in a different way?' or 'I dislike that kind of slang. It
makes it all sound so ugly. Are there any other words you
could use?'

The questions that young people ask at puberty make
it very obvious that many do not have the basic language
they need to talk about their bodies or about sex. When
they have the freedom to ask questions about what they

really want to know, they are incredibly honest. I am constantly amazed at how quickly children open up and allow themselves to be vulnerable in front of other students. This is true between the ages of ten and eighteen. When young people feel respected, they treat the teacher with respect. When they know their questions and comments will not be judged, they have the confidence to be truthful. Younger children can reveal what they have been hearing from their friends. Older teenagers can talk about their experiences with the other sex.

The best time to help young people to make good decisions about their sexual behaviour is before they become sexually active. Around puberty is a good time to help them find the middle ground between promiscuity and the misguided isolation that makes for coldness and hardness. Good relationship education begins with honest communication. It is some consolation for the parents of uncooperative teenagers who refuse to communicate, to learn that at adolescence good teen-parent communication is far less important in influencing sexual behaviour than parental attitudes and supervision.

CONTRACEPTION

It is not my intention to shock anybody by writing about some of the questions children ask most frequently at puberty. Many of these questions are quite vulgar and shocking. They illustrate the confusion of children who are caught between repressive and permissive attitudes to sex. There is a great deal of confusion among young people, for example, about AIDS and the HIV virus. Common queries are: 'If you are having safe sex for some time and you want to have intercourse without a condom, how do you do it?'; 'How can you be a father if you have safe sex?'; 'Would you get AIDS from French kissing?'; 'If you had AIDS when you were having a baby, would your baby's children have AIDS?'

In a survey carried out in England for the television programme *World in Action*, ten-year-old children who did not understand the word 'contraception' were able to tell a researcher what a lady did if she did not want a baby. They knew about condoms, a tablet the lady takes when she does not want a baby, an operation and the female condom. Some children said women who did not want a baby used abortion, as if it too were a form of contraception.

Legal controversies about abortion have made Irish children very aware of what is involved in terminating the life of an unborn baby. Many children do not fully understand the advertisements they see and hear about 'safe sex'. It is not unusual for children to focus on the words they understand and get a distorted message. I remember meeting a woman whose ten-year-old daughter asked her, 'Did you and Dad have to practise sex before you were married?' A little probing elicited the information from the child that she had just watched an advertisement advising viewers to 'Practise safe sex'.

Young children need to be informed that a woman and a man who are virgins when they marry are not at risk. A woman who is faithful to her husband and he to her is not at risk of contracting an STD. This information would help to enlighten the many confused youngsters who do not understand that 'safe sex' advertisements are aimed at people who have more than one sexual partner.

CONFUSION ABOUT 'SAFE SEX'

Many young boys try to work out how you can be a father
if you wear a condom. Young people who have not yet
reached puberty have taken the 'safe sex' message to
heart. They have definitely got the message about pro-
tection. Unfortunately that message is not balanced with
similarly well-publicised information that encourages
monogamous relationships or reassures those who are
happy with platonic friendships. It is sad to find eleven
and twelve-year-old children who assume that it is normal
for adolescents to have sex. A common worry for boys
is: 'What if your penis is too small for a condom?'

Adolescents need balanced information about HIV and
AIDS. They need to be told, 'You do not get the disease
from being in the same room as someone who is infected.
You do not get it from door knobs or toilets or in
swimming pools. There are only four ways to catch the
virus. If a mother is infected and pregnant she will pass
the virus on to her unborn baby. The virus is also passed
on through infected blood. It was passed on through
blood transfusions before blood was heat-treated. Intra-
venous drug abusers pass on the virus when they share
needles. When couples exchange bodily fluids through
having sex, they can pass on the virus.'

Children need to be reassured that their parents are
unlikely to be at risk. They need to be told that these
advertisements are not aimed at faithful couples. It may
be necessary to explain that 'safe sex' advertisements are
for people who have more than one partner. Teachers

need to be prepared to deal with questions from children whose parents may be engaging in risky behaviour. Children are often aware when a parent is having an affair. They usually know when there is marital conflict.

A question like, 'Miss, you know when your Dad has a row with his girlfriend and he goes off and sleeps with someone else, could he get AIDS?' needs very delicate handling. Once it is asked and the family situation is revealed in class, the question cannot be withdrawn. Other children in the class may be affected by stories of family conflict. Some children may become unduly upset when their parents have a row in case they too will separate.

Some teachers are reluctant to focus on the importance of monogamy for fear of giving offence to children or parents. This need not be a problem if delicately handled. It is not difficult to help children understand that we all know the ideals we should live up to, but all of us fail to do what we know we should do. By using examples that are meaningful to the lived experience of the children in a class, it is possible for a teacher to model respect and tolerance.

PEER-EDUCATED CHILDREN HAVE UNNECESSARY WORRIES

Boys need a lot of reassurance about the size of their member. 'If a penis is very small does it mean that you are not going to have a child?' They need to know that the size of a penis has no bearing on whether a man can give his wife pleasure in marriage. They also need accurate information about nocturnal emissions. Peer-educated children are often left with the worry that they will wet the bed when they have a wet dream. Boys are notorious for exaggerating. Let them know that the semen will leave just a slight stain on their pyjamas that is easily cleaned.

Once hormonal activity begins young people are fascinated by who does what and to whom. Some of the most frequently asked questions about intercourse are: 'What age should you be to have sex?'; 'What would happen if you had too much sex in twenty-four hours?'; 'How long does it take to make a baby?'; 'Would your foreskin be ripped back when you have sex?'; 'Does sex hurt?' Although the majority of young people are fully aware that it is illegal to have sex with a girl who is under seventeen years of age, this does not preclude questions about underage sex.

AT WHAT AGE?

It is impossible to answer a question like, 'What age should you be to have sex?' without clarifying what it is exactly the young person wants to know. Saying something like, 'I'm not sure I understand what you are asking me?' encourages the younger child to be more specific. It may be a question of clarification on what is the legal age for sex. On the other hand the 'should you be' is often indicative of peer pressure and may really be a plea for reassurance about delaying sexual activity. There is great consolation for young people who are reassured in a group or class situation. It breaks the sense of isolation that 'I am the only person who feels like this.'

Such questions give adults wonderful opportunities to use reflective listening and give young people accurate information based on sound moral and spiritual values. I suspect that they are more likely to reveal their curiosity about such matters to a visiting teacher than to a teacher they meet on a daily basis. In sexual matters young people say it is easier to admit to curiosity with a stranger than with someone familiar.

Curiosity about how long people spend making love is common. Some questions can be answered by simply saying: 'There is no special length of time that a couple would spend in lovemaking. How long intercourse lasts is a very personal matter. Does that answer your question?' Worries about damaging the penis and about sex hurting are also common. Young people need to know that sex is a pleasurable event for both the woman and the man. An inquisitive youngster who wants to know about having too much sex needs good listening. 'What do you think yourself?' or 'I wonder where you heard that?' are questions which encourage the child to open up and allow the adult to find out what the girl or boy believes.

TALKING TO TEENAGERS ABOUT HAVING SEX

Be positive and give accurate information when teaching about sex. Tell the children that having sex is wonderfully pleasurable and creates an emotional experience that bonds the couple in love. A couple who are virgins when they get married can enjoy discovering the joys of sex with each other. Every girl and boy deserves to have a memorable first sexual experience. If the relationship is casual and there is no long-term commitment, the conditions for lovemaking are less than ideal. If one partner is more sexually experienced it may lead to feelings of inadequacy or fears of comparison. After casual sex it is not uncommon for one or both people to feel guilty and worry about the possibility of pregnancy.

To have a romantic and guilt-free experience, honest communication is necessary. I tell young people that couples who cannot speak openly about their expectations of a relationship have no business being intimate with each other. Freedom from guilt or shame is an essential prerequisite for entering into the delights of enjoying togetherness in sexual intimacy.

Good sex needs honest communication and the freedom to talk about what kinds of caresses and touching one likes and does not like. The couple who are virgins when they marry have the comfort of learning together. Knowing that their sexual performance is not going to be compared to other lovers is helpful. Monogamous couples are also protected from health worries about STDs. There is no denying that some people have sex in the absence of a loving or committed relationship. Young people often argue that this is all right if both of them agree. This attitude needs to be challenged by both teachers and parents. The fact that two selfish people agree to use each other for sexual thrills does not make it right.

THE HEALING POWER OF SEX

Sex gives an illusion of intimacy that can easily be mistaken for true love. Young people need to have factual information about the emotional and spiritual consequences of casual sex. Genital intimacy transforms the relationship. It creates emotional closeness and a deep desire to be acknowledged as special by one's partner. The power of sex to heal old hurts is deeply spiritual. Good sex is a truly blessed experience that changes the relationship radically. Properly used, it has great potential to heal. When it is misused it can do enormous damage and wound people deeply. Sexual feelings are very exciting and to be enjoyed, but they do not have to be acted on. Adults cannot emphasise enough that acting on sexual feelings is a life-changing decision.

HOMOSEXUALITY

In a caring, sensitive listening environment young people can be encouraged to explore their own values and attitudes. Young boys tend to worry more about their sexual orientation than young girls. It is sad to find young people so sexualised before they reach puberty that they are worried about being gay. Common questions are: 'What is a homosexual?'; 'Is there anything seriously wrong with gays?'; 'How do gay people make love?'; 'How does a man become gay?'; 'How does a woman become a lesbian?'

It is helpful to ask, 'I wonder where did you hear that?' If children ask a question I believe it is best to give them some information. 'A homosexual is a person who is sexually attracted to a person of the same sex. It could be a man who is attracted to another man or a woman who is attracted to another woman.' Hurtful terms to describe homosexuals are still in common usage. Children often use them without realising this. Prejudice is learned and is often nurtured in families.

To an adult a question like, 'How do gay people make love?' may be taken as an enquiry about anal intercourse. Have no doubt that some children know exactly what is going on. They use terms like 'bumming' and 'backshafts'.

It is best not to answer questions like this without checking them out. 'I'm not sure I understand what you are asking me' may elicit a very different question. 'Johnny told me that in Denmark gays kiss each other and hold hands in public. Is that true?'; 'If gay men kiss each other would they get horny?'

Great sensitivity is needed by a teacher or counsellor who is answering a question like, 'Is there anything wrong with gays?' Some parents are tolerant and accepting of minority groups. Others are prejudiced and intolerant. Ideally teachers will be guided by a school policy that clearly sets out the agreement with parents on how these matters are to be presented to children.

APPROPRIATE LANGUAGE

The terminology used for intercourse can also be quite crude. Adults have to take some responsibility when children speak in vulgar terms about sexual matters. A very popular fortnightly British teenage magazine illustrates a different position for intercourse in every issue. The difficulty of the position is graded between one and five. Is it any wonder that children at puberty are looking for information on the different positions for having sex? Many know more about sexual variety than their parents.

They are curious about orgasm and how couples make it happen. Frequently children do not have the correct words for body parts. Their questions are crude and vulgar. 'If you were having sex would you stick your prick in her hole once or stick it in and out all the time?' Encourage them to rephrase such questions. 'It is understandable that you use those words. Can you remember the more grown-up names for the genitals?'

KISSING

The slang terminology used by young people to describe kissing is not unlike the Eskimo language with its many different words for snow: 'Frenchie', 'shift', 'snog', 'shifting', 'meeting', 'tonsil hockey', 'getting off' and other vulgar terms that it would serve no good purpose to print in a book. Some terms are peculiar to particular regions. Kissing terminology also goes in and out of fashion.

No parent or teacher is expected to be familiar with all the terminology young people use. It is not unknown for children in a class to test a teacher by making up something and asking for an explanation. It is only sensible for a teacher who does not recognise a word to be honest. 'I haven't heard that word before. What do you think it means yourself?'

Never give children wrong information if you do not know what they are talking about. The unsavourily named 'black kiss' had its origins in miscommunication between adults and children. Young people who knew a 'rainbow kiss' was one of the slang terms for oral sex were given wrong information. They were told it meant kissing a girl during her period. The school-yard sex gurus put two and two together and came up with distorted information, a 'black kiss' – oral sex during a girl's period.

OTHER QUESTIONS

When children ask questions they are usually seeking accurate information, reassurance or moral guidance. Quite often they need all three. I find that parents tend to treat girls and boys differently where sex education is concerned. Girls are more likely to be educated about the facts of life than boys. I suspect this is due to the fact that girls avidly read teenage magazines and are more likely to discuss what they read with their friends. Here is a small selection of questions frequently asked by pre-pubescent children:

- 'What are hormones?'
- 'What is a gynaecologist?'
- 'Boys have erections when they see a sexy girl. What do girls do when they see a sexy man?'
- 'Do you start using deodorant when you get your period?'
- 'Boys have wet dreams. Do girls have them too?'
- 'If you drink when you are pregnant would it harm the baby?'
- 'Do boys get cranky during puberty?'
- 'What happens to a woman who can't have babies? What's wrong with her?'
- 'Is it right to go with a boy that is younger than you?'
- 'If a girl is fun to be with and has a good sense of humour should you ask her out?'
- 'What does "pure and untouched" mean?' [Eleven-year-old girl who looked up 'virgin' in the dictionary]
- 'Do you know the white stickiness in your pants? Does it continue after your period?'
- 'Is your foreskin joined to your penis? Is it meant to be?'
- 'Parents think twelve-year-olds should not be dating. Are they right or wrong?'

- 'I am nearly twelve. Is it illegal to have sex?'
- 'Is it normal to feel tingling in your private parts when a sexy play or film comes on TV?'
- 'Can you get pregnant without having sex?'
- 'What is fingering?'
- 'What's a blow job?'
- 'What's a lick out?'
- 'What's a sixty-niner?'
- 'Do couples lick each other in sex?'
- 'Is masturbation bad for you?'
- 'What is a diddy wank?'
- 'What's a wanker?'
- 'What does shagging mean?'
- 'Why does a girl's vagina sweat?'

ABSTINENCE MESSAGES

It must be obvious that many of the children who ask these questions are as much in need of reassurance and guidance as of accurate information. It is only to be expected that some unhappy teenagers who feel unsupported by parents may decide to use the closeness of sexual intimacy for comfort and affection. It is widely accepted that a great deal of teenage sexual activity occurs because young people do not know how to meet their need for love in any other way.

If school-based sex education programmes are to be effective they need to combine clear messages about sexual behaviour with strong moral and logistical support for the behaviour sought. It takes self-confidence to refuse unwelcome sexual advances. Those who come from troubled families (this could be as many as one in four families) are more likely to engage in early sexual activity.

Young people need to hear that there is nothing wrong with them if they choose to delay becoming intimately involved in a couple relationship. Many need the reassurance that delaying sex does not reflect a low sex drive but rather indicates that a young person has the control which is so important for sensitive lovers to develop.

PRIMARY SEX EDUCATORS

There are lots of young people who feel trapped between their own desire to delay intimacy and the peer pressures that make them behave like their friends. Teachers have the power to educate young people to think about their choices. It can be a very powerful learning experience for them to look realistically at the long-term consequences of their decisions. This option is less likely to be rejected when it is openly discussed in a classroom situation.

Teachers can correct wrong information and ensure that young people are educated to have a realistic understanding of the processes involved in building a long-term, stable, monogamous relationship. Many young people consider that their parents have a boring relationship. They need to understand that the early euphoria of falling in love does not last indefinitely. The excitement of young love alters over time. It becomes deeper, and though less passionate, it is still a fulfilling experience when couples retain good communication.

There is no doubt that the relationship of parents plays a very important role in the way young people first develop a sense of self-esteem. The foundation for good self-esteem and the way children learn to relate is laid in the home, not in the school. Teachers build on the foundation laid by parents. Research shows that knowledge alone does not have a measurable impact on sexual behaviour. Family relationships do. No matter how skilled teachers are in giving RSE they can never play more than a supportive role to the parents. Children will model their relationship behaviour on how they see their parents act rather than on what they are told they should do.

10

'SEXPERTS' GET THINGS WRONG

AVOIDING QUESTIONS

I was pregnant with my third child when my eldest daughter Aileen was four years old. She asked me: 'How will the baby come out?' I was so poorly informed about sex education that I believed it was not wise to answer questions like that from a very young child. I decided she did not need the information until much later. I said, 'I'll tell you when you are older.' That was the best answer I could give at the time. A few months later she got the mumps and I had to call the doctor. I still hold the memory of her sitting up in bed. Her cheeks were puffed out and she looked sick and miserable, but she said, 'Doctor, I have a question to ask you. My mammy doesn't know the answer.' I knew what was coming. 'How do babies get out of a mammy's tummy?' The doctor looked at me. I trusted his knowledge and expertise in these matters. I said, 'You explain.' He thought for a minute before he answered. 'Well, Aileen,' he said, 'it's very hard to explain to a little girl but I'll tell you what. When you grow up you can be a nurse and come to the hospital with me and I'll show you.'

When I was in hospital after the baby was born she tackled her dad. He avoided giving her an answer too. He said, 'The nurse took Mammy into a special room called the delivery ward. Your little sister was born in there. I didn't see what happened.' She was not satisfied with that answer either. As soon as I came home she brought the subject up and again I failed to give her correct information. 'I couldn't see how the doctor got the baby out. My bump was in the way,' I said, fudging the issue. Is it surprising that she never again asked a single question about pregnancy or childbirth? I made a mistake when I failed to be open with her. I had the best of intentions based on my desire to do what was best for my child, and I got it wrong. The result was that she learned certain questions were taboo in our family.

ACCURATE INFORMATION DOES NOT DESTROY INNOCENCE

I was brought up to believe children should not be told 'these things'. When our doctor avoided the question his response confirmed me in the decision I made. If my daughter had let the issue drop and not continued to ask, I might have forgotten the incident. However, she kept asking for the information she needed. I consulted some friends and enquired what they would do in the same situation. Every one of them felt she was too young to have an answer. Yet it continued to bother me. My child asked the same question, time and time again over a period of months. Deep inside I knew she needed an honest answer but I did not have the self-confidence to go against expert advice. I was scared to trust my own instincts.

Few young parents have the appropriate language to explain to their children about childbirth. When I told my daughter where babies come from, I said, 'The baby grows from a little seed inside the mammy's tummy.' She was happy with that for only a few weeks. It was a measure of my naïveté that I was totally unprepared for further questions. It should have been obvious that any intelligent child would want to know 'How did the baby get in there?' and 'How does the baby come out?' Looking back, it would have been so easy to tell her but I simply did not have the confidence or the language to do so.

I must have been crazy to believe that accurate information would steal my child's innocence. Like many new mothers I looked to professionals and experts to advise me on what was in the best interests of my child. I was taught to trust doctors and priests, who were better qualified to know about these things than ordinary people. I looked to them to tell me what to do. I turned my back on my own very powerful maternal instincts. I was reluctant to give sex education because I felt confused and uncomfortable. To talk about sexual issues to a child I needed a lot more information on the subject.

FINDING ANSWERS

Over twenty years ago I set out to teach myself about giving sex education. I was determined not to leave my daughters sexually ignorant. I wanted to discover the kind of answers that were appropriate for the questions children ask at different stages of their development. I started by going to my local library to look for books on sexuality. The first thing I discovered was that I was badly in need of sex education myself. I assumed that I would find two or three books by different authors that would tell me what to say to my daughter and how to say it. I could not have been more wrong.

I assumed experts shared the same basic theories and philosophy about sexual matters. I was surprised to find they did not. I was even more surprised to find so many different religious teachings about sexuality. It was astonishing to discover that not alone did the experts have different ideas, but they also contradicted each other and offered conflicting advice. When you stop to think about it, it seems obvious. Psychologists, sociologists and educators are doing research all the time. This means they are coming up with new ideas. It is only natural that sometimes these new ideas will conflict with older, previously accepted ideas.

'SEXPERTS'

It was no great surprise to discover that much of the research on child-rearing practices conducted during the 1950s and 1960s was based directly on Sigmund Freud's psychoanalytical theory. This emphasises the effects of early feeding and toilet training experiences. A lot of the information generated from this research contributed to our understanding of sex-role development in children.

What was startling was the discovery that the work of Havelock Ellis was much more influential than that of Freud, who is regarded as 'the father of twentieth-century sex'. Ellis was an English doctor who later turned to the study of psychology. He challenged the attitudes of guilt and fear about sex that were prevalent in society in the

1890s. He also accepted deviations from the norm that would still be controversial today. He tolerated masturbation, homosexuality, and what he came to see as a natural interest in sexual variety. He did not approve of traditional Western marriages. He believed marriage might need to be augmented by some type of sexual variety to keep it alive.

Most people are aware that Freud wrote extensively about sexual development. I am not so sure that they are equally aware that many eminent psychiatrists, doctors and educators disagree with his theories on the early developmental needs of children. He labelled the stages of psycho-sexual growth as the oral, anal, phallic, latent and genital stages. Freud shocked the public with the suggestion that the oral, anal and phallic stages concerned infant sexuality. The latent stage was a period of inhibited sexuality. He believed that at the time of puberty sexuality blossomed and he called this the genital stage. Modern sex educators disagree with his ideas about a latency stage.

Alfred Adler was a colleague of Freud. He worked with him for six years before moving on to work out his own theories. Adler had a student named Viktor Frankl – the famous psychiatrist who spent three years of his life in Nazi concentration camps. Frankl went on to develop what he called 'the third Viennese school of Psychotherapy'. Adler and Frankl had similar attitudes towards sexuality. Adler recognised two phases of sexual development – the first a biological phase, the second a social phase.

Adler wrote: 'Love, as a task of two equal persons of

different sexes, calls for bodily and mental attraction, exclusiveness, and a total and final surrender. Sexuality becomes mature when it becomes a task for two, when it becomes social rather then biological.' Frankl wrote: 'Normally sex is a mode of expression for love. Sex is justified, even sanctified, as soon as, but only as long as, it is a vehicle for love. Thus love is not understood as a mere side-effect to sex, but sex as a way of expressing the experience of that ultimate togetherness that is called love.'

Freud made the world aware of the fundamental importance of sexuality in the life of a person. Many very eminent psychiatrists and psychologists believed he misinterpreted the value and significance of the affectionate and social side of people's sexual lives. Not alone did these men disagree about the aims and purpose of sexuality, but they did not even understand the word 'sexual' in the same way.

THE KINSEY REPORTS

Halfway through the twentieth century, in 1948, the famous Kinsey report on male sexuality was published. Five years later, in 1953, the report on female sexual behaviour followed. For the first time ever, people learned about the intimate sexual practices of women and men in the United States of America. They discovered what other people did in bed. Kinsey found that women who considered themselves virgins had a lot of sexual experience. For example:

- 100 per cent kissing
- 74 per cent deep kissing
- 72 per cent manual stimulation of the breast
- 32 per cent oral stimulation of the breast
- 36 per cent received masturbation
- 24 per cent performed masturbation
- 17 per cent contacted bare genitals with their own
- 3 per cent received oral genital contact
- 2 per cent performed oral genital contact

Alfred Kinsey spent twenty years studying gall wasps before he undertook the study of human sexual behaviour. He believed that if animals did something, humans did it too. In some ways animal sexual behaviour became the model for human sex. He wrote: 'The elements that are involved in sexual contacts between the human and animals of other species are at no point basically different from those that are involved in erotic responses to human situations.' He believed that it was our attempt to distance ourselves from our mammalian ancestors that caused us to take sex out of its natural context.

MASTERS AND JOHNSON
In the 1960s the pioneering work of William Masters and Virginia Johnson provided further factual knowledge about sexual behaviour and brought in the feminine balance that was lacking in previous research. Their research indicated that sexual problems were a part of many if not most relationships. Not alone did their work offer hope to people who were suffering from sexual problems, it also provided vitally important medical information about sexuality.

EXPERT THEORIES AND SEX EDUCATION

The names of Freud, Adler, Frankl, Ellis, Kinsey, Masters and Johnson are now known all over the world. Yet they represent only a fraction of the number of experts who have written about sex and sexuality. Even a cursory glance at their work makes it obvious that there are many different theories about sexuality. Put quite simply, it seems that renowned experts have opinions that have been well thought out and apparently verified by their research findings. It takes a long time for such findings to be accepted by the public. Once accepted they are very influential and hard to dislodge. Accepted theories continue to influence people's sexual behaviour long after they are disproved by scientists.

Has this any relevance to giving sex education to children? A little, but it is much more relevant to the sex education of adults. Research information is used to devise educational policies and to give advice to parents. It is even utilised in the making of legal decisions affecting parents and children. As new research evidence is verified, older theories need to be revised, updated or even acknowledged to have been incorrect. It takes a very long time to bring new information into the public arena *even when it is shown that the original research was inaccurate or misleading.*

It is possible to find scholarly or research data to prove or disprove any point you want to make about sex education. There is some research evidence to suggest that well-informed teenagers are more likely to postpone sexual intercourse and be more responsible generally in their sexual behaviour. I am sure there is equally valid research to prove the opposite. I have no doubt that those who are against giving sex education to children could find a substantial body of research evidence to support their viewpoint. In this book I have used studies and research findings with which I agree and which confirm the points I want to make about relationships and sexuality education.

DANGERS OF LOOKING TO THE EXPERTS

I know there are many well-intentioned parents who regard psychologists, sociologists, counsellors and teachers as experts. Even when they are uncomfortable about the suggestions they make, they feel they should follow their advice. I know this only too well because I have done so myself. It is understandable that many adults do not feel well-educated in sexual matters. They feel inadequate because of their perceived lack of knowledge. One result of this inadequacy is that they look to the experts to tell them what to do. Many people go along with what 'sexperts' suggest even when it means denying their own bodily experience. Because of Freud, women reported experiencing two kinds of orgasm for generations before Masters and Johnson proved that all female orgasms follow the same physiological patterns.

Now I am not for a moment suggesting that the advice of professionals who have a lot of expertise should be ignored. Of course it is important to be aware of what renowned experts write and teach. But it is equally important to listen to your own feelings and trust your own instincts. Be wary of giving the opinions of experts more credence than your own opinion. Parents are the experts where their own children are concerned. Most parents trust the advice of experts because they have been taught to depend on authority figures for guidance rather them on themselves. They could be better off if they trusted themselves and made the decisions that they felt were right for their family.

CONDITIONED TO DENY OWN EXPERIENCE

From an early age children are programmed to distrust their own feelings. They are taught to check things out and ask for permission for almost everything. Parents decide what clothes they can wear. Teachers even have power over when they can go to the lavatory. While it is necessary to have rules to protect young children, those who learn to check everything out when they are young are conditioned as adults to look to others for guidance. They are programmed to trust the experts' ideas rather than their own opinions. As a result they are more open to peer and media influences. Adolescents who have been taught to accept rules unquestioningly learn to look outside themselves to discover what is appropriate behaviour. Some will go against their own feelings and reject their own ideas rather than be seen to think or act differently from their peers. The fear of being rejected because one is seen to be different is too much for most people to cope with in a mature way.

Research shows how simple it is to get people to deny the validity of their own experience in order to be agreeable. In one experiment that proves this, twenty-five people are brought into a room. They have only one task to perform. They will be shown two lines A and B on a television screen and they have to decide which is longer. They are allowed time for discussion before they make a decision. It sounds simple but there is a catch. Twenty out of the twenty-five people are plants. They have been told to say that the shorter line is the longer one. They have even been rehearsed so that they sound convincing.

When the two lines appear on the television screen first, the five unsuspecting people say A is longer than B. The other people disagree and claim that the opposite is true. They are definite that B is longer than A. The five independent people begin to doubt the evidence of their own eyes. When an open vote is taken the twenty plants declare that B is longer than A. It is found that the other five people agree that this is so. This experiment has been performed with many different groups of people and similar results have been obtained.

Isn't it true that many adolescents find themselves in a similar situation to the five independents? They set out wanting their first sexual experience to be with someone very special. The dream of falling in love, getting married and living happily ever after is shared by many outwardly tough teenage girls. Their friends dream differently. They talk about 'living happily ever after' if the relationship works out. When marriage is not seen as a desirable option by their friends, young people change their ideas. Anyway, most have seen too much marriage breakdown to believe that marriage is the key to a longer lasting relationship. It is understandable that so many young people feel it is better for a couple who are in love to live together first to test the stability of the relationship.

Separating sex from intimacy

Society's attitude to 'living in sin' has totally changed in the last half-century. The problems of marriage break-down have become so acute in modern society that many people favour trial marriages, with the idea that if they do not work out, they are spared the trauma of separation and divorce. If the couple find that they are happy living together and decide to have a baby, then they may consider getting married. Yet the figures for marriage break-down among couples who have lived together before tying the knot are surprisingly high. It is too early to say if this is because people who have the freedom to live together are more likely to have the freedom to walk out on the relationship if things are not going well. It may also have something to do with a reluctance to be tied down in a committed relationship.

Adolescents have never before been so vulnerable in sexual matters. The language of sexuality has been usurped, with many modern young people thinking of sex as meaning genital expression. They have grown up in a sexually permissive society and have been peer-educated to isolate sex from intimacy. They are desperately in need of positive teaching that will encourage them to celebrate who they are as sexual people. We have seen that young people will never learn to deal with their sex drives until they become familiar and comfortable with their own sexual responsiveness. To do this they must have access to accurate information when they ask for it. Without adequate encouragement and support they can very easily be pressurised into premature sexual activity. If parents and teachers fail to educate them to be sexually mature they will be street-educated by peers as ignorant as themselves. It is hypocritical to tell young people that they are too young to have sex if at the same time parents and teachers are unwilling or unable to educate them to be sexually assertive.

FEELING USED

Young people instinctively know that something is wrong when sexual activity creates distance rather than intimacy. Kissing, hugging and embracing are appropriate ways of showing physical affection that lead to intimacy. They are the easy parts of affectionate love. Young people need the reassurance of knowing that they have intimacy needs that can be met through physically affectionate friendships without having genital sex. They need to be aware that when there is a sexual relationship without commitment they run a serious risk of hurting themselves physically, emotionally and spiritually. Even very young children are aware of the risks of contracting STDs. However, the emotional and spiritual hurt that is caused by feeling used and exploited instead of bonded and emotionally healed and sustained is not so widely recognised.

Too many young people have been deprived of this information. They have never been made aware that sexually permissive behaviour is a way of avoiding intimacy. Those who are sexually active eventually realise that genital sex in the absence of an exclusive committed relationship does not bring intimacy. Instead it leads to a sense of isolation and feelings of being used. These feelings often bring shame, guilt and other painful feelings.

SEX IN MARRIAGE IS BETTER

Studies done at the Kinsey Institute show that sex in marriage is more satisfying than extra-marital sex. This is because sex within a committed exclusive relationship is more likely to meet the human yearning for intimacy. It fulfils the desire to be recognised as special in a most satisfying and pleasurable way. It opens up communication at the deepest possible level between a woman and a man. It bonds them together in a mutually pleasurable experience that is energising and lifegiving. It heals and transforms in an intensely pleasurable way.

Effective RSE will encourage young people to see how the choices they make about their sexual behaviour are influenced by their family, their peers, society, religion and the media. Understanding is the key to changing attitudes and behaviour. Adolescents must be challenged to think for themselves about the long-term consequences of the choices they make. It is only through their own insights, and not through the imposition of parents' or teachers' values, that they will come to understand what it means to be a healthy sexual person. In the process they will need to examine and question the status quo.

If parents and teachers are defensive or unprepared for this questioning process it is inevitable that young people will look elsewhere for information. Television is recognised as the sex educator of the 1990s. The World Wide Web information network on the Internet is likely to be the source of information in the next millenium unless the attitudes of parents and teachers change radically.

There is no argument about the need girls and boys

have for sex education. The ideal is for children to live with two parents who respect and care for each other. Parents who model loving communication to each other and to a child teach children about faithful, monogamous relationships. Unfortunately not all children have the advantages of an ideal family situation. Unless school-based educators grasp the nettle and design programmes that acknowledge and examine relationship problems, children who live in unhappy family situations are put at a disadvantage.

By the time young people reach puberty they are the experts who can tell parents and teachers what they need to know regarding sex and sexuality. If they are allowed to ask questions in the knowledge that they will be answered without judgement or condemnation, they will be educated to understand what is required to work at sustaining a relationship. The secret of ensuring that children get the best relationship education is to acknow-ledge the influence of their primary carers. Adults need to listen and give them clear, factual, holistic information when they ask either implicitly or explicitly.

Adolescent girls and boys need to be educated to understand that when they become parents they are likely to do to their children what was done to them, unless they make a conscious decision to do otherwise. They need to be educated about the hurt that is caused when people fail to communicate honestly. Few families enjoy the kind of communication skills that lead to this kind of open-ness. Older parents are not to blame for this. They did not have the benefit of the new psychological insights that can do so much to improve family relationships. Younger parents do, and this opens up new choices for them regarding sex education.

One of the most carefully evaluated courses in sex education took place at Grady Memorial Hospital in Atlanta, Georgia. Researchers found that: 'Formal sex education is perhaps most successful when it reinforces the behaviour of abstinence among young adolescents who are practising that behaviour. Its effectiveness diminishes significantly when the goal is to influence the behaviour of teenagers who are already engaging in sex.'

The reality of life today is that young people who do not value virginity have no intention of saving sex for marriage. The majority of parents have reservations about this change in attitude, for many different reasons. Although the desire to encourage young people to postpone sex is deeply felt, there is a widespread reluctance to stress abstinence messages. I suspect parents are not aware of the studies that show that these messages help young people delay sex. They also have an impact on the behaviour of students who later engage in sexual intercourse. They are more likely to use contraception.

It is up to the parents and teachers of this generation to break the taboos on talking about sex. It is only in this way that they will effectively educate young people about the physical, emotional and spiritual aspects of sexuality. Surely young people deserve this.

BIBLIOGRAPHY

Adler, Alfred. *The Sexual Function: Superiority and Social Interests.* Evanstown, North-Western University Press, 1964.

Bausch, William J. *Becoming a Man.* Connecticut, Twenty Third Publications, 1988.

Bennett, Dr David. *Growing Pains.* Northamptonshire, Thorsons, 1987.

Berne, Eric. *Games People Play: The Psychology of Human Relationships.* Harmondsworth, Penguin, 1969.

Clarke, Keith, Capuchin. *An Experience of Celibacy.* Notre Dame, Ave Maria Press, 1982.

Collins, Pat, CM. *Intimacy and the Hungers of the Heart.* Dublin, Columba Press, 1991.

Dickson, Anne. *The Mirror Within: A New Look at Sexuality.* London, Quartet Books, 1987.

Dillon, Valerie Vance. *Becoming a Woman.* Dublin, Columba Press, 1990.

Dominion, Jack. *An Introduction to Marital Problems.* London, Fount Paperbacks, 1986.

Frankl, Viktor. *Man's Search for Meaning.* New York, Washington Square Press, 1965.

Gaffney, Maureen. *The Way We Live Now.* Dublin, Gill and Macmillan, 1996.

Goergen, Donald. *The Sexual Celibate.* London, SPCK, 1976.

Gray, John. *Men are from Mars, Women are from Venus.* London, Thorsons, 1993.

Herron, Aidan and Dominic McGinley. *Tell Them.* Dublin, Mentor Publications, 1987.

Humphreys, Tony. *Self-Esteem: The Key to Your Child's Education.* Middleton, Carrig Print, 1993.

Kohner, Nancy. *What Shall We Tell the Children.* London, BBC Books, 1993.

Kramer, Dr Jonathan and Diane Dunaway. *Why Men Don't Get Enough Sex and Women Don't Get Enough Love.* London, Virgin Books, 1994.

Kinsey, Alfred. *The Sexual Behaviour in the Human Male.* Philadelphia, W. B. Saunders Co., 1948.

Kinsey, Alfred. *The Sexual Behaviour in the Human Female.* Philadelphia, W. B. Saunders Co., 1953.

McDowell, Josh. *Why Say No to Sex?* Eastbourne, Kingsway Publications, 1990.

MacNamara, Angela. *Ready Steady Grow.* Dublin, Veritas Publications, 1991.

Masters W. and V. Johnson. *Human Sexual Response.* Boston, Little Browne, 1966.

de Mello, Anthony. *Awareness.* London, Fount Paperbacks, 1990.

Mussen, Paul Henry et al. *Child Development and Personality.* New York, Harper and Row, 1984.

National Marriage Guidance Council. *Sex Education in Perspective: A Symposium on Work in Progress.* Rugby, 1972.

Nelson, Richard. *Human Relationships Skills, Training and Self Help*. London, Cassell, 1990.

Pearsall, Dr Paul. *Super Marital Sex, An Important New Study of Sexuality*. London, Ebury Press, 1988.

Pickering, Lucienne. *Boy Talk*. London, Geoffrey Chapman, 1992.

Pickering, Lucienne. *Girl Talk*. London, Geoffrey Chapman, 1992.

Powell, Elizabeth. *Talking Back to Sexual Pressure*. Minnesota, Compcare Publishers, 1991.

Quinn, Michal and Terri. *What Can a Parent Do?* Dublin, Veritas, 1986.

Quinn, Michal and Terri. *Parenting and Sex*. Newry, Family Caring Trust, 1991.

Reinisch, June with Ruth Beasley. *The Kinsey Institute New Report on Sex*. New York, St Martin's Press, 1990.

Satir, Virginia. *Peoplemaking*. Palo Alto CA, Science and Behaviour Books, 1972.

Spock, Dr Benjamin. *Bringing up Children in a Difficult Time*. London, New English Library, 1977.

St Clair, Miriam T. *The Vice of Today*. Limerick, City Printing Co., nd.

Skynner, Robin and John Cleese. *Families and How to Survive Them*. London, Mandarin, 1989.

Tannen, Deborah. *That's Not What I Meant*. London, Virago, 1992.

Tannen, Deborah. *You Just Don't Understand*. London, Virago, 1992.

Valles, Carlos G. *Courage to Be Myself*. Anand, Gujarat Sahitya Prakash, nd.

Walker, Richard. *Sex and Relationships: The Complete Family Guide*. London, De Agostini, 1996.

Whitehead, Evelyn Eaton and James D. *A Sense of Sexuality*. New York, First Image Books, 1990.

Articles in Newspapers, Magazines and Journals

Andrews, Paul, SJ. 'The Tasks and Pitfalls of Growing Up'. *Studies*, 81, 324, Winter 1992.

Argyle, M. et al. 'The Communication of Inferior and Superior Attitudes by Verbal and Non-verbal Signals'. *British Journal of Social and Clinical Psychology*, 9, Part 3, September 1970.

Coldrey, Barry. 'The Sexual Abuse of Children'. *Studies*, 85, 340, Winter 1996.

Gaffney, Maureen. 'Adolescence and Family Conflict'. *Studies*, 81, 324, Winter 1992.

Irish Times, Saturday 16 July 1994.

Miller, B. C. and K. A. Moore. 'Adolescent Sexual Behaviour, Pregnancy and Parenting: Research through the 1990s'. *Journal of Marriage and the Family*, 52, 1024-44.

Whitehead, Barbara Dafoe. *Atlantic Monthly*, October 1994.